MW00640289

UNLOCK OVER $2K IN BONUSES

'isit **www.TheUltimateMarketingPlaybook.com/member**
today for free BONUS content & start dominating NOW.

Thank you for your purchase! You've
made a powerful decision to make
your business thrive and we have
the resources to help you, so you
don't have to do it on your own.
Get instant access now at:

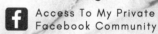
Access To My Private
Facebook Community

Exclusive Training
Series For Video
Mastery

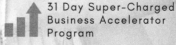
31 Day Super-Charged
Business Accelerator
Program

www.TheUltimateMarketingPlaybook.com/member

The Ultimate Digital Marketing Playbook for Dominating

Your Local Area:

Take the Guesswork Out of Digital Marketing, Maximize Profits and Become the Authority in Your Business or Profession..........

Even in a Bad Economy

By Krista Mashore

ACKNOWLEDGEMENTS

I'd like to sincerely thank all of those great professionals who were interviewed for this book. Some are students of mine and others are just awesome professionals in their field that I highly respect. If you ever need their particular type of service, please contact them and tell them "hi" from me!

Carol Delzer: Family Law Center, Sacramento, CA.; www.FamilyLawCenter.us; author of *Divorce Done Easier* and *Eight Weeks To Collaborative Co-Parenting For Divorcing Parents*

Debbi Galvan: Land Home Financial Services, Concord, CA.; www.LHFS.com

Glenn Hoffman: Discovery Bay Insurance Services, Discovery Bay, CA; www.DiscoveryBayInsurance.com

Nina Koch: East County Performing Arts Center, Brentwood, CA.; www.BrentwoodDance.com ; author of *Bella Bunny*

Tiffany Rose: Guild Mortgage, Walnut Creek, CA.; www.GuildMortgage.com

Tracie Schmidt: Supreme Lending, San Diego, CA.; www.tracieschmidt.supremelendinglo.com

Carol Van Bruggen: Foord, Van Bruggen & Pajak, Sacramento, CA; www.FVBE.info; co-author of *It's Not About Your Money, It's About Your Life*

AND MORE THANK YOU'S...

I first want to thank all of you who have taken the time and belief in this book (and me) to pick it up to read. Coaching, training and inspiring people is the love of my life. I have never felt so much joy and felt so called to do anything as much as I do that. So, thank you for allowing me a piece of your time and attention. I promise not to let you down.

I want to let my husband Steve know how much I appreciate his support and devotion to our marriage and family (you are my favorite, yes even more than my dad). He is so loving and always assists me with my crazy ideas. You are my forever!! Nothing will ever tear us apart.

To my kiddo's, Jaynlin and Kayli, you are my world and I am proud of you both. When I see your loving, giving hearts, it makes me know that I've done an amazing job as a mom. I couldn't love or be prouder of you. And to my bonus son, Casey, thank you for giving me a chance, I'm so proud of the young man you are and continue to become.

I couldn't love my family more, Dad and Mom, your love and support and high moral compass has helped me become the woman I am today.

Lastly, and so importantly, my amazing team. All of you have worked so hard and given your all. I know at times I can push too much, but I never question your loyalty and dedication to our cause. Because of all of you, we are building Community Market Leaders across the country who are Go-Givers and who are making an impact on their communities. Thank you for helping be a part of this national movement we are creating. I love you all as dearly as family!! A special thanks to Chrissy, Meaghan, Athena, Jaynlin (my amazing marketer) and my amazing editor, Heather.

What Our Past Clients are Saying About US...

Eric A. "Not only has Krista's coaching helped immunize my business from the coronavirus, it's actually thriving more than it ever has in my three years in the industry. Jan-April 2018 income this time last year (prior to Krista's strategies) in a strong economy: $9,554.21. This year Jan-April 2019 income (post Krista) in a worldwide pandemic: $54,939.50, which is a 577% increase YOY."

Leslie B. "Blown away!! Y'all, I did about $5 Million (2018) in volume last year. This year (2019) I did over $15 Million in volume in my little county of only 44,000 people. In 2017 I made $12,175.00. In 2018 I joined Krista's program in April, I ended the year doing $135,768.10. I continued to implement her strategies in 2019 and ended my year grossing $353,135.60 which is a 1,115% increase from 2018 to 2019."

Alex M. "Our less than 2-minute video got almost 72 hours of watch time in only two and a half days, and I've gotten 8 referrals adding up to 12 new contracts in a two week period."

Jennifer P. "Wow, this Krista Mashore seems to know what she's talking about. In the last 7 days I've had 55,248 people see my ads and only spent $179.67."

Alisha C. "2017 I closed 105 transactions. The first 12 months of implementing her out of the box techniques, I did 171 transactions, that is 66 more than the previous year. The numbers just came in for 2019 and we did 293, that is 188 more transactions in 21 months.

My first year implementing Krista's strategies my business increased by 191%, and a 146% increase the second year."

Erica W. "Before implementing Krista's strategies, I was averaging 40 transactions. Last year because of the innovative strategies that I learned, I closed 70 transactions. My income increased by $203,000. That was a 175% increase in transactions. Also, my average sales price was 400K and now my averge sales price has increased to 700K."

Debbi G. " I had only closed on 6 clients from Jan to April, after implementing Krista's strategies, I closed the year out with 74 contracts/clients funding over 30 Million in contracts."

Jen H. "It took me a little over a year for my last website to start showing up in searches, but here I am already coming up 5th on two searches. Krista Mashore your program rocks!!! If you're new, just do what Krista teaches and be patient. The results will come!!!"

Heather W. "Such an amazing Summit. There was so much fabulous content that I could immediately implement in my business!! Absolutely worth the investment!!"

Tammy V. "I am doing the full coaching program and so far it's the best money I've ever spent on coaching. The content, how-to's, written scripts, CRM flows and community give you more than you could possibly imagine. Considering my last coaching experience was the price of a college education, Krista Mashore is worth at least triple what they charged."

Sue L. "This has been the most incredible journey for me! This program has changed my life, my career, and I can't begin to tell you all the lifelong friends I've made here."

Dave N. "Received a call from my dental office and the receptionist said, "I have been seeing your videos on Facebook a lot lately and my daughter is needing your services and is going to hit you up."

Fran D. "I'm sold on Krista's strategies. I created my first lame video and ran an inexpensive Facebook. Received 20 leads and they keep coming in."

Chelsea C. "This program is absolutely amazing! Just yesterday from one strategy taught in the program, I was able to pick up 5 new clients!! There are hundreds of strategies taught in the program. Trust me you want to join this coaching program. Krista Mashore is amazing!!!"

Tina M. "I love Krista's training. I was in her 3 in 30 days training class and it was amazing. I got 3 new clients from it and one even gave me a referral."

Jen H. "It took me a little over a year for my last website to start showing up in searches, but here I am already coming up 5th on two searches. Krista Mashore your program rocks!!! If you're new, just do what Krista teaches and be patient. The results will come!!!"

Shemika F. "I am a true believer in this program and forever grateful for all that I have learned. My business and confidence and content are continually growing, and I feel authentically connected to my mission and business."

Pat H. "So looking forward to 2020 with all the tools, education and support of the Mashore Tribe. I have been growing and I can't keep up. Got recognized for the Presidents Club Award, $22 Million in Sales Volume and 72 units."

Dana C. "On one ad I had 1,805 people watch the entire video and on the other I had 2,194 people watch the entire video and only spent $75.00 on each ad."

Julee P. I went from averaging around 20 to 25 deals a year, to 47 and my team did 62 (and I didn't have a team prior) which is a 248% increase in business.

CONTENTS

INTRODUCTION

This will be the fourth book I've written within the last two years. Crazy, right? Let me tell you I did *not* decide to write this book because writing a book is so fun and easy. It isn't (at least not for me) and fitting it all in while maintaining my real estate business and growing and scaling my coaching business, well, my husband will tell you (as he's told me) that no sane person would put so much on her plate.

But my coaching clients and students kept bugging me to do it.

See, I wrote my first book, *Sell 100+ Homes* based on my real estate expertise and the new ways of doing business I'd developed that were totally non-traditional—and awesomely effective! I started coaching other Realtors® in these same methods and saw them achieve incredible results. Not only were they more successful financially than they'd ever been, but they were happier and more satisfied with their lives in every way.

Then I started coaching people who were not Realtors® and saw them achieve incredible results as well. It turns out that the strategies I teach can be successfully applied to *any* type of business. These clients urged me to do a book for people who wanted to start their own businesses. So, I did. It's titled *F.I.R.E.: Your Crappy Job Won't Quit Itself.* Then, because I'd been interviewing all of these absolutely amazing top professionals and businesses across the country who had so much great stuff to say, I decided to put those interviews together in a book. That one's called: *3 Clients in 30 Days.* Two of these books have become national and international bestsellers on Amazon.

Then my students with careers in various businesses and professional services started achieving incredible results. The thing I've noticed with many businesses and professionals is that they've trained and educated themselves, sometimes for many years, for a certain career such as in law or healing or finance. But it never occurred to them that they had to create a *business* around that career. And for some of them, even just hearing the word "digital marketing" would give them the heebie geebies. They're brilliant and talented and knowledgeable, but they weren't able to achieve the success they wanted to achieve—until they started learning and working with these strategies.

I will never know as much as you do about your business or profession. I don't know how to write an insurance policy, make a latte or draft a family trust document. I could never advise people about how they should set up their retirement funds or what kind of emotional counseling they need. But here's what I *am* an expert in: helping people to apply specific cutting-edge practices and to implement a business model based on core principles to become as successful and fulfilled as they choose to be, in whatever business or profession they're in.

As in just about every industry, the old traditional models are no longer working. For many businesses' or professions, the internet has become big competition. We've got online mortgage lenders, do it yourself online wills and trusts, even medical information on the internet. The industry and your client base are changing, and you need to change with them. That may sound scary, but . . .

What if you no longer had to chase down clients but clients actually came knocking at your door?

What if you no longer had to go to every networking event in town to get a few measly referrals but created an ongoing stream of clients who were exactly the kind of client you want to work with?

What if your clients trusted you and felt comfortable with you before they even met you?

What if you had so much business every month that you could easily afford the help you need?

What if you were able to call the shots when it came to how much income you would make, how many hours you put in, and how you spent those hours?

What if you started to really enjoy your work again and that spilled over into making the rest of your life happier and more relaxing?

Sound impossible? Here's what Kim Renshaw had to say after implementing this program for 18 months: "I was looking at my stats the other day because I'm a numbers girl. I haven't even implemented all parts of the program, but I realized that I've closed almost as much in six months as I have in my best year. If you do all of the foundation work, then the rest of it just starts coming. I still have a lot more to implement from the program. I'm just excited to see where it takes my business."

Tracie Schmidt, a loan officer with Supreme Lending who is also in my program, agrees, "Now I'm just more confident. I'm closing eight to ten deals a month when before I was closing two to three, and people are just wanting to know what I'm doing. That's the biggest thing that this has done for me is exposure. It's people calling me really wanting to work with me, thinking they *have* to work with me. I'm not chasing after clients anymore."

Right now, you're probably lost in the big field of others who are in your field— whether it's chiropractors, architects, or business consultants—who are *not* offering as much value to their clients as you can. To be seen as a leader in your industry, to be relied upon, respected, trusted and valued, you have to give exceptional value! You have to do things differently. You have to be smarter! You have to be innovative, use technology, and apply specific principles and practices of leading Fortune 500 Companies.

You have to offer services that are *game changing*, not just adequate.

If you ask old trainers and coaches in your industry (who are often teaching and coaching because they themselves couldn't make it in the business), they would tell you that what I'm teaching is *not* how it's supposed to be done and it will *not* work. Yet it's succeeding, every single day—not only for my students and coaching clients but for zillions of people in all kinds of industries.

It's succeeding through the art and science of what I call Engagement Marketing (Chapter Two), which is one of the most powerful tools you can learn. It's succeeding through folks becoming Community Market Leaders™ (Chapter One) and implementing the principles that Community Market Leaders base their work on. It's succeeding through the *proper* and *strategic* use of the engine of the internet and social media and the secret weapon that makes it mega-powerful (Chapter Three). It's also succeeding through the *different* approaches I'll show you in branding (Chapter Four), customer service (Chapter Seven), and effective goal setting (Chapter Ten).

I'll also show you the *mindset* (Chapter Eleven) you'll need to go from a career that is plodding along and life that is "just okay" to a career that is fantastic and a life that is amazing!

Who the Heck is Krista?

I did *not* start out as a hot shot career woman running huge businesses. Twenty years ago, I was a 3rd grade teacher. I loved the kids and loved the teaching, and I was really good at it, even going for my Masters in Curriculum and Instruction. But I decided I wanted to spend more time with my young girls so I got my real estate license (honestly, everyone seems to have one in California!) and left teaching so I could be at home and just "play at real estate" on the side.

Well, you know what they say about the best laid plans.

It happened on a Saturday. I was at breakfast with five of my girlfriends and all our kids. We had all gone to high school together and our children were growing up together. We were having a great time, laughing, reminiscing, with the kids all running around. It was like your perfect Saturday morning. My phone rang and, being a new real estate agent at the time, of course I answered it. A friend of mine from college was on the other end and she told me she had just seen my husband in Napa. I said, "Oh yes. He's there at a golf thing for work." She paused then said, "No Krista, I'm so sorry but, I saw him being intimate with another woman. Something's going on, Krista."

My heart started racing and I could feel my face flush. Tears instantly welled up in my eyes. I was hit with hurt and anger and an instant, crazy loop in my head: "But, we have kids. We built this life together. How many more lies did he tell? How could he be so foolish to throw this all away?" Even worse, I felt humiliated because this was not the first time and I was angry at myself for "allowing" it to happen again.

I remember driving home from the restaurant, doing my best to hold back the tears so that my daughters couldn't see, but before I could even really wrap my mind around what was going on, I knew I was going to have to save myself. More importantly, I knew I was going to have to take care of my daughters and give them the life they deserved. I didn't know what that was going to look like. I mean I had just left my safe, secure full-time job as a 3rd grade teacher. I didn't know what was going to happen next or how I was going to handle it, but I remember a little voice saying, "You know Krista, your world is about to change drastically and you need to be ready for it."

In just a few moments, my world was gone, and I was at risk of losing everything. I panicked thinking I might lose my daughters, or they might not be able to live with me. I was freaked thinking my kids could lose their home, that they'd lose any sense of normalcy being thrown back and forth between their father and me. My life got so crazy. Within a week of my husband leaving me and tearing up what I thought was our happy home (I guess we all think that right before our world is torn apart!), I watched my two daughters being picked up by his new girlfriend who was driving *my* car! And my bank accounts were completely drained, and we just bought a new home. I mean who can even make up such craziness? Well, in a matter of days, this was my life.

Now I know some of you are thinking that everyone gets divorced, it's normal. Well, not for me, not for my family. My parents have been married for over 52 years and my brothers for 21 and 26 years. So, it was devastating to me. But in the midst of it all, I knew I needed to be able to support myself and my kids and give us a real life. It was up to me.

That realization propelled me into becoming the rookie of the year in my first year in real estate. It got me to work smart and hard, selling 69 homes my first year and averaging at least one hundred homes every single year thereafter. It was the motivation that built my business and put me in the top 1% of all Realtors® in the nation. Not because I wanted to, I mean my goal was to "play real estate" not to be thrown into survival mode.

So, I built my first business based on survival. But my second business, coaching and training, was built from passion.

In 2017, my real estate business was booming. I had done exceptionally well through tough markets and good markets. I had remarried to an amazing man who is also a terrific father to my daughters. My girls were old enough that they were almost ready to be launched into lives of their own. I should have been blissfully happy and grateful, and I was. But I also felt a nagging feeling of wanting to do something more.

I knew how awesome all the strategies I'd learned over the years were. They not only helped me in my own career but had helped others that I'd trained and mentored along the way. Because I love to learn, I'd attended tons of seminars and workshops over the years, picking up all kinds of insight, information, and wisdom. I have a passion for teaching. I have a passion for giving back and helping others. And I knew that, by sharing what I know, I could help others achieve what they wanted to achieve as well.

Unlike you, who probably have zillions of hours of training in your business or profession, I had *no* idea how to become a trainer and coach. You definitely have a leg up on me in that regard. Yet I knew I had the tools to make any kind of career successful. So, I pulled up my Big Girl pants and decided to launch a training and coaching business. And by following the principles I'll share with you in this book, I built that business very quickly.

Can it really happen for you?

Let me give you an example: Cassie Spears has been in the real estate business since she graduated high school. Within the first few months of being in the program and using the strategies in this book, she picked up six new clients and 13 new property management deals. People were seeing her out there. Her business exploded so much in the first six months of being in the program that her husband quit his full-time job even though he was in a professional job and made really good money. From January until August, Cassie had already done the same amount of business that she did the entire year before. She said, "I've learned so much more in this past six months than I had in eighteen years." Cassie had been doing business the old-fashioned way, and that's what's happening with most industries. Loan officers, insurance agents and financial advisors, you name it. They're still doing business the way they were taught so long ago.

But once you read this book, you'll know there's a better way.

The fact that you've picked up this book tells me you are committed to success. It also says you are open to coaching and learning. So, let me start by coaching you on how to get the most value possible from this book.

Getting the Biggest Bang Out of This Book

I'm going to cover a ton of information over the next several chapters. I'll teach you several specific tools and techniques my students and I have used to create amazingly successful businesses. Then I'll show you how to stay on top of these new tools (which can change daily if not hourly!). I'll give you some exercises and assignments to sharpen your skills, and I'll give you links to resources you can check out. And while it's great to read a book and gather information, the key is to *implement* what you learn. As my clients and students will tell you, taking action is where the gold is.

Some people like to take it a chapter at a time, stopping after each chapter to put the recommendations of that chapter into place. Others read through the whole book to get the lay of the land. Either way is great. However, be sure not to stall out after implementing just a few chapters. All of these tools work together so you'll at least give *all* of them a try and not just pick and choose a few. If you're reading through the whole book first, be sure to go back and do the work. Go back to the beginning and work through it step by step! Knowledge is just the booby prize and you won't see results if you don't put it into action.

Mastery, implementation, and consistency are so key. Be a *doer* not just a thinker. You've spent hours and hours perfecting your craft. Now it's time to spend some time making sure your professional life becomes as successful as you want it to be. Apply the principles, master them, don't give up, be consistent. Have "definiteness of purpose." In *Think and Grow Rich*, Napoleon Hill wrote, *"With the proper desire and definiteness of purpose, i.e. consistency and a 'never give up attitude,' you will end up succeeding."*

Will you need to do things differently than you've done them before? Absolutely! Will you go through a learning curve where you feel like a raw beginner again? Most likely. Will you need to step out of your comfort zone sometimes? Absolutely. Will you see results immediately? Maybe. But, by staying consistent and focused, as my clients will tell you, you'll definitely see great results over time.

How do you climb Mount Everest? One step at a time. In fact, climbers who climb that huge mountain take *very small steps very slowly*. They know that it's more important to keep going than to sprint and burn out before they get to the top. So just keep moving forward. You'll get to the top of whatever your Mount Everest is.

I didn't start out doing everything in my business the way I do it today. Over the years, I improved, innovated, tried some things that worked and others that didn't. I just kept going. One step at a time. I have spent hundreds of thousands of dollars —I kid you *not!*—and thousands and thousands of hours learning and trying things that simply did not work. I've taken all the knowledge, training, trials, and errors and created a system and way of doing business that *does* work.

Here's an important key: Even though I've been in the Top 1% in the U.S. in real estate, I *continue* to sharpen and change my skills on a *continual* basis as technologies change in that profession. I do the same in my digital marketing training business. Even though I've generated Four 2-Comma Club Awards in a 19-month period, (each digital funnel generating over 1 million dollars in revenue)

I'm very clear that I need to stay fresh and innovative, and to stand out from the pack. (In fact, my editor has started complaining: "Krista, please stop evolving and learning new information so fast so we can at least get this book done!") As soon as my competitors start doing what I've been doing, I'm already on to the next idea, staying five steps ahead of the curve. This isn't done by luck or chance. I do it by constant education. I focus on what is relevant in my industry right now as well as paying attention to what I see coming down the pike based on my research.

My goal is for you to be successful, whatever that means to you. I'm going to give you the success strategies, the mindset, the approach, and the specific tools that I use in my own professions and that my clients now use in theirs. I'll illustrate how effective these tools have been through stories from my clients, as well as stories from some other professionals and businesses I highly respect who have used this same approach to become leaders in their field. In my own case, by applying what I'll teach you here, my training and coaching business has grown from zero students to over 650 in less than two years and the business is now generating around $3.2 million annually.

And that's not luck, my friends. That is not luck. It's following the exact same principles I'll teach you in the next chapter and applying those principles systematically in my businesses.

Take the Next Step

1. *Stop right now and pull out your calendar. Schedule enough time to read at least 10-15 pages of this book every day for the next few weeks.*
2. *Grab a stack of sticky notes. Whenever you run into a good thought or new idea, mark the page it's on so you can go back to it.*

CHAPTER ONE

BECOMING A COMMUNITY MARKET LEADER

I mentioned that one of the cornerstones to the methods I teach is the focus on becoming a Community Market Leader™. You're probably wondering, "What the heck is that and why should I care?" Here's my definition of what Community Market Leader™ means:

> *"Domination of market share within a specific geographical location, accomplished by **excellence** in education - which really is marketing - innovation, technology and engagement. A leader that serves and makes a contribution to our community. CMLs create more financial freedom, time, and a healthy work/life balance. We have abundance in all facets of life. As market leaders, we pledge a solemn promise to our clients, and to ourselves, to give nothing other than one hundred percent in all we do with the utmost integrity."*

A Community Market Leader: Not Just One of the Pack

So, what does it mean to be a Community Market Leader™ in your field? You probably have examples all around you. It's the person you instantly think of whenever you're looking for an expert in a particular field. "He's got the pulse of everything happening." "She's got such a solid reputation." "He's the one whose face you see all over town, the person whose name everybody seems to know." It might be the person you hear being interviewed on local radio or TV as an "expert commentator." If you're in a field that tracks such things, the Community Market Leader® is the person who regularly ranks #1 or wins awards for their work. They are the person your see volunteering and giving of their time. They are focused on giving back to their community and making a difference.

I'm that person as a Realtor™ in my community. My student Tracie Schmidt, a loan officer with Supreme Lending, has become that person in mortgage lending in San Diego. My client Alisha Collins has become that person in real estate in Wyoming. I want to teach you how to become that person in your market.

My success and my coaching clients' success in dominating our markets didn't happen by luck or accident. We're all smart and determined, but so are you. It takes some specific actions and skills to get into that Community Market Leader™ position, all of which I'm going to show you.

First, let me be clear, I didn't follow the same playbook that traditional real estate agents or people building coaching/training businesses follow, and I don't teach my clients to follow the traditional playbooks of their own industries. I learned early on that if I wanted extraordinary results, I had to be different than the others. I had to come up with innovative ways of marketing and running my business. I had to eliminate traditional practices that *didn't* work and *improve* traditional practices that *did*.

For example, when I first started 18 years ago, I invested in high quality, full color, four-page brochures instead of flimsy, cheesy one-page flyers. Before the days of Zillow and individual real estate marketing sites, I put small CDs out as "virtual tours." I also marketed my listings on television. To stand out from the crowd, I had to stretch personally and professionally, see things from a different perspective, and push myself through any fear or self-doubt.

And you will have to do the same in your field. Years ago, Nina Koch, dance instructor and owner of East county Performing Arts Center and Boogie Babies Dancing Studio in Northern California, tried something no one had ever done in her community. She convinced the local newspaper to insert a flyer about her programs. "Honestly, the flyer was pretty awful, and I didn't know what I was doing. But I wanted to try something new that no one else had done. And as soon as the insert came out, my phones were ringing off the hook and I had more students than I could handle!"

Even if you're already good at what you do, I believe there's always a better, more effective way to do almost anything. That's why I push myself and my clients toward continual educational. That's why I dive into situations that might stretch my thinking and challenge how I do things. Learning even one small thing each day will keep you expanding into the next "better way." More importantly, you need to implement that better way and continue to improve on it.

> *Learning even one small thing each day will keep you expanding into the next "better way."*

Basic Principles

Being a Community Market Leader™ is based on some core themes and you'll see them repeated throughout this book, over and over again. Why? Because they're so critical. I use them in *every* aspect of my business, and throughout this book, I'll be showing you how other businesses and professionals have applied them to their careers to create phenomenal success. These basic principles aren't just a nice sounding philosophy. These principles actually show up in a tangible way in everything I do and in everything the other businesses and professionals mentioned in this book do.

The first theme is to **go above and beyond** in everything you do and even in how you think. The question can't be, "Did I do enough?" It needs to always be, "What more can I do? How much more value can I add to anything I touch or anyone I interact with?" A Community Market Leader™ focuses on the most she can do, not the least she can get away with.

Another core principle is to **use the power of technology**. I used to get freaked out by technology and think it was beyond me. Today, avoiding technology isn't really an option for any of us. The power of technology and the millions of ways you can use it will make the effort to get comfortable with it totally worthwhile. You can (and should) use technology for everything from sending video emails and text messages to keep in contact with clients to processing whatever information or records you need in your field. You can (and should) use technology to keep your team organized, to post informational videos on social media to your target market and to keep contact with existing and potential clients with CRM (client relationship management) software. *Every* part of your business will be better when you get innovative with technology.

Which brings me to **being innovative**, doing whatever you're doing in a way that's different than the way others do it. For example, I create educational videos about current topics and distribute them on multiple platforms to ensure maximum visibility. I design landing pages and use "pixels," which is a targeting system that monitors the behavior of online users, and re-targets and markets to them in the future.

Being innovative involves using technology, but it's more than just technology. For instance, say you're giving a talk at a local event. You could just show up with a Power Point and spout out a bunch of information. Or you could actually create some kind of interactive workshop where listeners could experience what you do. You could send them home with additional resources or some kind of checklist like, "How to Talk about Finance Before Tying the Knot" or "Six Things To Know Before Designing Your Dream House."

I can go on and on about how you can stand out and change things up based on what's happening in your market and in your industry. With all aspects of your business, you need to be thinking, "How can I do this differently? How can I do this better than everyone else?"

Becoming the authority is another theme that is critical to my success and will be critical to yours. It's beyond being an expert in your field. You need to be *known* as the *authority* in your field, the go-to person. You need to be tracking trends and new discoveries in your business or profession. You need to offer cutting-edge practices in your field. You need to continually educate yourself and do research to stay current. But here's the key: You become an authority when people *know* that you're an expert. If no one knows you have all that expertise, it does you little good. Think about why you picked up this book. It's most likely because you see me as an authority in marketing and building your business. Something I've done has caught your attention. I'm not only an expert, but an authority that you want to get advice from.

An integral part of being an expert and using your expertise to become an authority is to **educate others**, not only your current clients but your entire community. This doesn't mean slapping together a newsletter that gives a bunch of statistics nobody understands or cares about. A Community Market Leader™ uses his or her expertise to truly educate people in meaningful ways. A chiropractor might send out brief videos on what kinds of school backpacks are best for kids' postures. A mortgage lender might send out a video explaining how a first-time buyer can prepare credit-wise to get a mortgage. An attorney could shoot a video on the most important things to put in a rental contract. You need to be intentional about what you're putting out there and be service-oriented, not robotic.

By sharing your expertise, you **build trust** with your clients and the broader community. Think about it: How important is trust to the relationships you have, whether personal or business? If you're like me (and almost everyone else on the planet), it's huge. Building trust is a skill and intention every Community Market Leader™ must have. I'll show you several highly effective ways to develop trust throughout this book. It's not just something that's nice to do—it's an absolute *requirement*.

Part of building trust is showing your community that you really know what the heck you're doing. It's also about being impeccably ethical in all you do, even if it means losing business. I *never* fudge the rules for a client or colleague for self-serving interests, and I lead my clients in a manner that will guide them to their best possible outcome, not mine. If something doesn't serve the client, if it doesn't serve the community, then it doesn't serve me.

One of my mottos is, "Make good choices even when no one is looking and always have integrity." I used to say this to my kids every morning. If I forget to say it, they'd yell it over their shoulders as they ran out the door.

"Make good choices even when no one is looking and always have integrity."

I incorporate that saying into my everyday life, both personally and professionally. If impeccable integrity is not something you think you can live with, I'd suggest you stop reading and return this book for a refund because everything I teach is based on this principle.

Which brings me to another core theme that has played a tremendous role in my success: **an attitude of service**. When my coaching clients really get and apply this principle, they're astounded by the results it brings. It seems almost counter-intuitive, but the focus is *not* on selling anybody anything. It's on giving your clients and your community real value in everything you do. It's keeping your clients' best interests in the forefront, giving them everything they need and more than they expect.

Based on this attitude of service, I don't show up saying, "Hey, look at me. I'm hot stuff. You should work with me." I show up saying, "How can I help you? How can I be of service to you? How can I add value to you?"— and I mean it. This ends up translating into a ton of business coming my way. Just as important, it lets me sleep well at night! I've come from an attitude of service for years in real estate, and I approach my training and coaching business with this same attitude. I was put on this planet to serve, to be of service, and to give back. It's about how much I can *give*, not how much I can get. My saying is, "People before things. Take care of people and the things just come."

"People before things. Take care of people and the things just come."

15

And if you do all of that—be totally trustworthy, become an expert and educate people with that knowledge, use technology effectively, stay innovative, and always go above and beyond with an attitude of service— you'll end up **being unique**, my last core principle. To be a leader in any kind of business, you need to stand out from the pack. You can't just do things or think the way everybody else in the crowd does. You need to step into your personal strengths rather than trying to be somebody else. If the top loan officer in your firm is super-analytical, you can learn from that. But at the end of the day, if that isn't you, if you're more of an outgoing and enthusiastic person, emphasize those qualities. As an attorney, you might be very warm and humorous at times while the lawyer next door is Mr. Methodical. You can both do a good job for your clients, but you'll always do a better job and you'll get much farther for yourself and others by being *you* than trying to be someone you aren't.

I'm crazy hyper, fast paced, and energetic. You either love me or you hate me. I choose to associate with people and clients who appreciate my uniqueness, not those who want me to be someone else. I didn't feel this way when I started in business. I thought I had to look and talk and think like everyone else in my industry. Once I got over that, once I accepted myself for who I am, and focused on my unique strengths, my life and business became a lot more fun.

What You'll Get by Applying These Principles

As a Community Market Leader™, you'll find yourself no longer chasing after clients. As you'll see through the stories in this book, clients will seek you out. You will attract them.

You'll be able to develop the kind of business that best suits you and your lifestyle. If you want to be #1 in your field, you'll have the skills to do it. If you want to spend more time with family, you'll be able to take your foot of the gas without destroying your credibility.

If you want financial freedom, you'll be able to build it. Even if your goal is not to become #1, you'll be able to increase your business and have a more constant revenue with fewer ups and downs.

When you step into being a Community Market Leader™ in any business or profession, business is easier because it becomes like clockwork. It just becomes part of who you are. As you start to build a stable and profitable business, you can hire good people—specialists in every part of running your business— to help you.

Clients and others in the community will know and trust you. You'll be seen as the go-to person. Very early on in my coaching business, I got a call from a loan officer who said, "Krista, I see you absolutely everywhere. I just passed a billboard with you on it. I see your videos on Facebook every day. Everybody seems to know you. Whatever you are doing, and can you teach me how to do it?" I told her I was just starting to coach people and she said, "Sign me up!" We had never even met! Yet, she was immediately willing to sign up for my coaching because she recognized me as a Community Market Leader™

As a Community Market Leader™, I continually educate myself so I'm abreast of what's happening, whether it's in real estate or my coaching business. Whenever I do a speaking engagement or make a presentation, I'm completely confident that my information is rock solid, my methods work, and my recommendations are backed by research. I know that what I offer is cutting edge and effective. I know I can offer my clients more value than they ever hoped for. I want you to feel that way too.

Take the Next Step

1. *Think about people in your field that you recognize as being Community Market Leaders™. What are they doing? What makes them stand out?*

2. *Now envision yourself as a Community Market Leader™. What are you doing? How are you relating to your community and your clients? What is different than who and how you are in your business today?*

CHAPTER TWO

ENGAGE YOUR COMMUNITY

After getting all the training and credentialing they need, too often new businesses and professionals simply throw up a shingle and wait for clients to come flooding in. When that doesn't work, they go to workshops telling them to "sell yourself" to get business (which makes most of us cringe, right?). Well, I'm going to ask you to stop that. Just stop it! What you want to do instead is "serve, don't sell." Though I wish I had invented this concept, I didn't.

The "serve, don't sell" philosophy is used by many business giants you know, like Whole Foods, Apple, and Ikea. Business gurus call it "relationship marketing" or "content marketing." I call it "engagement marketing" because the focus is on engaging your community. (You may not even know who "your community is just yet but hang in with me.)

You don't have to take my word for it. Do your research. This type of marketing is the new "new" of best practices. Down the road, someone will undoubtedly come up with another best practice. My goal is to be the first in my area to adopt these best practices and apply them. It's your job too, if you want to have consistent income and clients flocking to you. Right now, that best practice is engagement marketing.

Engaging people, creating a relationship with them doesn't happen just

> *My goal is to be the first in my area to adopt these best practices and apply them. It's your job too*

by sending out post cards or a newsletter every month. It doesn't happen by putting an ad in the local paper with a discount coupon. To establish true connections and relationships and to engage people in your community, you need to go deeper, get more creative, and offer more value than that.

In the good old days, real estate agents used to hit the golf course to schmooze and "build relationships." I've seen financial planners and business consultants trolling networking events with the specific purpose of giving out zillions of business cards to anyone they could corner. I've seen chiropractors give "wellness seminars" that just turn out to be sales pitches for their own services.

The practice of engagement marketing is nothing like that. This quote from Oracle Marketing Clouds' website is a good description:

*"Relationship marketing is a strategy designed to foster customer loyalty, interaction and long-term engagement. It is designed to develop strong connections with customers by **providing them with information directly suited to their needs and interests** and by promoting open communication."*

Here's an even clearer explanation from *Youtility* by Jay Baer:

*"What if businesses decided to inform, rather than promote? You know that expression 'If you give a man a fish, you feed him for a day; if you teach a man to fish, you feed him for a lifetime?' The same is true for marketing: If you sell something, you make a customer today; if you **help** someone, you make a customer for life. **In every business category, one company will commit to being the best teacher, and the most helpful.** And that company will be rewarded with attention, sales, loyalty and advocacy by consumers who are sick to death of being sold, sold, sold."*

As a Community Market Leader®, you're going to engage people and build relationships by offering your knowledge and outstanding service. And you're going to do it in a way that reaches zillions of people yet still has a very personal touch.

I know this works because I've done it and people I've trained have done it. When I show up to a listing appointment, people act like they've known me for years. Even if I've never met them, they treat me as a good, trustworthy friend just because I've offered tons of information and service through social media and other marketing avenues. When I do a phone interview with a prospective coaching client, sometimes the only question they ask is, "How soon can we start?" They've read my books or watched my free videos and already feel like I've already contributed to their success. They're fully engaged with me before I even open my mouth!

Glenn Hoffman of Discovery Bay Insurance Services, Inc. in the San Francisco Bay area tells a story that illustrates how this can work. "Ten years ago, I started working with tow truck companies with just two clients in that industry. I not only made sure to provide great service to those clients. I also participated in their industry events, not just showing up. But, like Krista says, I was being active and a good resource for them. Recently, I sponsored one of their luncheons for fifty people. When I stood up and looked around the room, I saw that 48 out of the 50 attendees were clients of mine! It was humbling. I told the two who were not clients, 'Hey, I'd love to work with you, but I don't need to tell you what I do. Just talk to the person sitting next to you and they'll tell you what I can do for you.'" And *that's* the power of engagement marketing.

Wouldn't you prefer to have a client show up to their first appointment with you totally trusting you and committed to working with you? When they already *know* the value you can give, that's what happens.

Here are four different definitions of "engage" and how they apply to being a Community Market Leader™: 1) *To occupy attention* (you get peoples' attention when you offer what they're interested in), 2) *To secure for employment or hire* (you definitely want them to engage you, right?), 3) *To attract or hold fast* (when you offer expertise and service freely, your community is not only attracted but loyal to you), and, 4) *To bind, as by pledge, promise, or oath* (you give your commitment to do your best for your community and clients).

How the Big Guys Do It

Top Fortune 500 companies have used this approach and you probably never even noticed it. They just seem to be good guys, giving great service and educating people while asking for nothing in return. They're marketing but you don't feel like they're pushing their product or services on you. They're giving you something of value and you appreciate it, and you appreciate them for giving it. And when it's time to buy something they offer, who are you going to think of first?

The majority of our most recognizable companies like Google, IBM, General Electric, Nike, Coca Cola, and Whole Foods use some form of engagement marketing. They show that they understand us and what we need. They educate us and offer value rather than spewing sales pitches at us. This is certainly more pleasant and it's also incredibly successful! If it works for some of the best companies in the world, it's worth considering for your business, right? So, how exactly do they do their engagement marketing? A few examples:

Whole Foods: Whole Foods does tons of education. They offer customers information on healthy living and eating. They give useful tips on how to eat inexpensively, and they create articles on how to feel healthier based upon what you put into your body. Each store has "Take Action Centers" which, according to their website, "*offer customers a wide variety of information on local, regional, national, and international issues of concern. Customers not only learn about important issues like genetic engineering, organic foods, pesticides, and sustainable agriculture, but we offer them the means to affect change by keeping them updated on new legislation and the tools they need to effectively participate in shaping those issues.*" How could you educate your community about something within your area of expertise?

Financial planner Carol Van Bruggen of Foord, Van Bruggen & Pajak Financial Services in Sacramento puts on educational luncheons for her clients and invites them to bring guests. She brings in experts and chooses topics that are very timely. For example, right

21

before the new tax laws went into effect, she brought in a couple of sharp tax experts to talk and answer questions. "No one was trying to sell anybody anything. We just wanted to give them important information that obviously was going to affect their financial futures. Do we get new clients out of these luncheons? Usually, but that isn't the point. The point is to be of service and give them something that is valuable to them."

Ikea: Ikea is known as "the king of content marketing." Ikea's president explains it this way: "*So, we really start with the customer, and try to see what's important to them… And then how can IKEA help them so that we are truly partners in making their life better at home every day.*" One of their surveys showed that 72% of people feel stressed on weekday mornings. So, Ikea created a whole website dedicated to tips on how to get your day off to a good start. Brilliant! Could you figure out the pain points in your community and offer solutions from the perspective of your business or profession?

Carol Delzer of Family Law Center in Sacramento specializes in divorce mediation. In the past few years, she's written several educational blogs, posting them on her website. "The blogs are on topics that are important to people thinking about divorce like how divorce anxiety in men may show up differently than in women, or how to co-parent collaboratively after a divorce. It's not always specifically about the law but it's all those issues that people divorcing will face. The thing about doing these blogs is that it makes me even more passionate about the work I do because I want to help people through these issues. It focuses me on a more global perspective of what I'm doing, not just the paperwork involved."

Coca Cola: Coca Cola's marketing hasn't been so much about education as about giving emotional value. One of their campaigns started in Australia in 2011. It's still going strong and has evolved over the years. For the original "Share a Coke" campaign, Coke replaced the label on their bottles and cans with "Share a Coke with" then a name in that country. It might say, "Share a Coke with Jim" in the U.S. or "Share a Coke with Nigel" in the U.K.

People went running out to find a Coke with their name on it and they bought Cokes with friends' names on them. Soon the whole thing went viral because people posted pictures online with their personalized drinks. People loved it and it established a real emotional connection with their customers. Emotional connection and even fun are great ways to engage people in the community. The key is to think about what your community really cares about and come up with an authentic way to connect on that level.

A woman in my program, Julee Patterson of Gateway Properties in Auburn, California near the community of Loomis created a fun video titled, *"How to Know if you're from Loomis, CA."* In it, she says things like, "You know you're from Loomis if you celebrate eggplant." "You know you're from Loomis if you're always late because of the train." "You know you're from Loomis if you still call that vacant building on Main Street 'the bread store.'" They are all inside jokes that anyone from Loomis would appreciate. It makes them feel part of a special club when they recognize what she's talking about.

Moxie Pest Control: Moxie Pest Control designed an attractive "infographic" of a 7 Step process that shows you how to check your hotel room for bed bugs. (The first step is to leave your bags at the door in case you need to make a quick getaway!) How valuable is that, especially to frequent travelers? You can just print the guide out and throw it in your suitcase. With this graphic, Moxie not only shows off their expertise, but also gives us something valuable for free.

Bryan Bowman has established himself as an authority on how to sell online. He gives away a free video series with tips and tricks about how to sell on Amazon *and* specifically focuses on how to drive traffic *off* of Amazon, so the seller is not so dependent on that particular platform. He's clearly responding to a problem that sellers have faced and finding a solution that looks out for their best interest.

Charmin Bath Tissue: Okay, this example is a little silly, but it worked! Similar to Moxie Pest Control, Charmin focused on a common concern for people: dirty public toilets. They developed an app call "Sit or Squat" that lets people check public restrooms in their area to see if they're clean or not. The idea is, if it's clean you can "sit." If not, you might want to "squat." Genius! It not only addresses a real problem but it's very funny—and humor is an awesome way to connect and engage with people.

Glenn Hoffman of Discovery Insurance Services in the East Bay pays for an automated system called Hearsay where he can pick up marketing pieces. "I've posted several of the Farmers' ads that I think are really funny. Yes, they're ads. But I do it because it's entertainment and funny. It gives people a chuckle and I think we all appreciate that."

Lays: Lays (which is a Pepsi Cola brand) used a different facet of engagement marketing. Lays got their consumers involved with a *Do Us A Flavor* campaign. They ran a contest with cash prizes for people to submit their ideas for new flavors for chips. Everyone who submitted an idea got a graphic of their idea on a bag of chips. Then Lays set up a Facebook page where people could vote on their favorite new flavors. The campaign was fun and got people involved and engaged. Could you do something like this?

I did a challenge for my real estate business on Facebook: "I need your HELP Friends and Family.....$100 Visa Card to the person who can design my next Billboard ad w/ a Catchy Slogan. Something memorable, like the ads we see for Chick-fil-A trying, where a Cow is telling people to Eat more "Chikin". Bring it on People!" I was shocked at the number of responses and, even better yet, the great ideas they came up with. One of these ideas became my billboard ad—"Krista, The Key to Sold!"—and I gave them the prize and recognized them in a post on Facebook.

That's the key to engagement marketing is to give the community something they want or need that adds value to their lives. When you

> *That's the key to engagement marketing is to give the community something they want or need that adds value to their lives.*

do this, they certainly don't feel like they're "being sold." You're not asking your community for anything back. You're just giving to them, making their lives a little bit better, by educating them, giving them valuable information, or even giving them a chance to laugh or use their creativity. When you do that, you develop a relationship. They feel comfortable with your motives and confident with your service.

Become the Expert to Become the Authority

Because you're reading this book, I'm guessing you're above average. But many people in every business or profession know just enough to get by. You know what I'm talking about, right? It's the insurance broker who barely passes the annual credentialing for new products. It's that psychotherapist who does his continuing education every two years but doesn't bother to look into current psychological research or new modalities. It's the teacher who got a credential back in 1985 but doesn't really like kids. They aren't incompetent (at least, not totally) but they haven't made the effort to stay on top of leading-edge practices in their fields.

Many businesses and professions require a heck of a lot of education and training, but some do not. For example, many people become mortgage loan officers because it has the potential to be highly lucrative and requires relatively little education. It's way too easy to get your certification to be a mortgage loan originator (MLO). In California, you have to take 20 hours of NMLS-approved classes (3 hours of Federal law and regulations, 3 hours of ethics, 2 hours in lending standards for the nontraditional mortgage product market and 12 hours of undefined instruction on mortgage origination). You then take a test, get registered, have a background test (where you do have to show up as squeaky clean), get a credit check and get fingerprinted. Bam! You're now perfectly qualified to advise people and walk them through what is probably the biggest financial investment they will ever make.

Really? In what universe? It takes over *500* hours to become a licensed *manicurist*! It takes about *4 to 5 years* to become a licensed plumber which includes classwork and apprenticeship. It even takes *60 hours* of coursework to become one of those H&R Block tax preparers. So, why does it take so little time and effort to become a loan officer?

For many other professions, it takes a *lot* of work to get your initial license or credential but then, except for some continuing education courses, you can pretty much skate. To become a real expert and a real authority, that's not enough. Ask yourself: "How have I expanded, improved, and evolved in my business or profession?" "Am I making strides to get better and more knowledgeable?" "Am I still doing the same things that I learned when I first got into this business or profession?" Please don't compare yourself with the businesses or professionals around you. If your goal is to be a Community Market Leader™ and create a business and life that is outstanding, you need to set your sights a lot higher.

And how many professions have had to overcome negative PR over the years? Lenders, securities brokers, chiropractors, business consultants—almost all professions have been tainted by people in them who took advantage of their clients or didn't create the results for clients that they promised. Maybe it's not fair but that stain gets spilled on everyone in the field.

The good news is that as soon as you actually run your career like a *service* business, go above and beyond, and dive in to become an expert in this field, and when you put that knowledge out there, you automatically earn respect from people. It happens quickly because you stand out as being different and as a leader in your field.

In his book, *Outliers*, Malcolm Gladwell claims that it takes 10,000 hours to become an expert. Think about it, that's around 10 hours a day for 1,000 days! Even if you have a lot of aptitude, Gladwell said in an interview, "The point is simply that natural ability requires a huge investment of time in order to be made manifest." The author of *So Good They Can't Ignore You*, Cal Newport, emphasizes that *how* you're using those 10,000 hours is equally important.

He says you need to push yourself to the very limits of your current skillset to really expand into expertise.

Can we agree that standard continuing education and even your hard-won education and training don't qualify you as an expert?

Personally, I'm comfortable defining myself as an expert, especially in my real estate business. I've worked in real estate for nineteen years. I've sold over 1,900 homes, averaging 100. homes a year. And even though I have all that experience, I still take a minimum of three to five webinar classes a week. Some of the classes help me track trends in real estate, business, or the economy. Others are about technology, marketing, social media, and digital marketing so I can stay on the cutting edge of marketing techniques. I push myself to take classes and read about whatever will enhance the value I can give to my clients.

I was heading to another out of town training a while back, and my dad said to me, "Why do you do all these trainings, Krista? You're already in the top 1% nationally." I said, "Dad, the reason I'm in the top 1% is *because* I'm doing these trainings." I

> *The second you stop learning is the second you lose your claim to being an expert and an authority.*

don't think he really got it. The point is, *you can never stop learning.* The second you stop learning is the second you lose your claim to being an expert and an authority. The world changes rapidly these days and you need to keep up with those changes to be an expert. This applies to any business, career or profession you can name.

What does this all have to do with engaging your community? It has *everything* to do with it! You can be the nicest person in the world, but the person your community will flock to is the one who has the expertise and who they see as the *authority* in your field. We all do that. We want to work with people we like, but when it comes down to it, we pick a dentist, a surgeon, even a manicurist based on their expertise, not just their personality, right?

You have to become an expert, so you have valuable knowledge to share with your clients and community.

When my father read my first book where I basically said the same thing, he highlighted it and said, "It's too much to tell people to take lots of classes and continuing educating. They'll starve to death because they won't have time to actually make any money." I respectfully disagree and my success and that of my students and other highly successful businesses and professionals proves the point. Once you stop learning and educating yourself, you stop growing.

Because I was an educator, learning is in my nature, so I love it, but it doesn't mean that it's easy for me. I actually have a learning disability. I use tricks and hacks to make it easier for me, so I'll enjoy it. If it's not easy for you, figure out a way to make it easy. Use audio downloads and audio books. Download Audible or another software. Listen to educational business and marketing books while you're getting ready for work or cooking dinner. That's what I do. I try to not waste any spare minute, even when I'm standing in line, or driving. It has helped me immensely.

Every business and profession has thousands of great resources for learning what is happening in their field or industry. Find yours.

Step Up and Stand Out as an Authority!

That said, it's not enough to be an expert. You have to let everyone *know* you're an expert. You have to become the *authority* in your community. And the way you do that is by using your expertise to educate, enlighten and give value to people through engagement marketing, just like the Big Guys.

A lot of businesses and professionals don't even try engagement marketing (or content marketing) through education because they think it takes too much time. It's true. It might take a little more time than you're used to, especially in the beginning. However, with a little practice and the tools I'll share in the next chapters, creating things like free reports and informational videos will become as easy as scrambling an egg, and you'll develop an efficient system to get them distributed. It's all worth it, because you're making a long-lasting impression.

One of my students, loan officer Tiffany Rose of Guild Mortgage, says, "I always decide the topic of my videos based on what's going on with my clients. If one or two or three of my clients are hitting the same issue or asking the same questions, I want to help spread the message and clarify whatever it is. For example, I had a lot of clients not understanding about conditional approvals. 'Your assistant keeps asking me for more papers, but you said my loan was approved.' So, I did a video to help people understand what a conditional approval really means. Then I spread it out to everybody in the community on LinkedIn, Facebook, Instagram and YouTube. I said, 'It's called conditional because there are still items that we need to double check. The underwriter feels very confident that there aren't any red flags in the file, but we need some verifications.'" This not only cleared up the issue for Tiffany's current clients but showed her community that she knew what they needed to know.

Fitness coach Amanda Russell heard from many of her fitness clients that they are strapped for time (Who isn't these days?!?) and having trouble fitting in an exercise routine. So, she created videos with time-saving tips like preparing quick and healthy meals, and easy exercises you can do while traveling. Joshua Latimer, who specializes in good content for online marketing, has written an eBook that gives local professionals strategies on coming up with content that is really relevant to their marketplace. He realized that too many professionals put out content that just doesn't really land with the people these professionals are trying to reach, which of course, doesn't get them the results they're trying to get. A local pizza shop did a video on how to make your own dough at home. A local clothing store created a lead magnet showing which types of clothing styles to wear to accentuate your figure depending on your body style.

As you continue to give value and educate people, offering them information they need to help them be more successful, happier or to make educated choices, your community will lock into you as the authority they want to work with. Yes, it might take a little bit longer to do this process than running an ad in the local paper, but you'll see how it really pays off once you've done it consistently for a while. You're not going to able to go anywhere without everyone knowing who you are. People will like you, look up to you, and trust you because you're giving them something they really want to know.

An article from Content Marketing Institute (http://contentmarketinginstitute.com/what-is-content-marketing/) stated:

> *"Our annual research shows the vast majority of marketers are using content marketing. In fact, it is used by many prominent organizations in the world, including **P&G, Microsoft, Cisco Systems, and John Deere**. It's also developed and executed by small businesses and one-person shops around the globe. Why? Because it works. Specifically, there are three key reasons — and benefits — for enterprises who use content marketing:*
>
> * *Increased sales*
> * *Cost savings*
> * *Better customers who have more loyalty"*

Engagement marketing is a part of developing trust from your community. People will want to work with you because they like you and trust you even before they meet you face to face. You've given them a lot without asking for anything in return. You're their go-to authority.

What information is useful to share? Like Tiffany Rose, you can get ideas from the questions your clients often have or the issues you see them facing. Like Carol Van Bruggen, you can look at current events like the tax laws changing, see what would concern your clients and give them information and solutions. Like Carol Delzer, you can use some of the pain points that we all have and give insight based on your profession.

Let's take stress as an example. Who doesn't have some level of stress in our crazy world these days? So how could you offer something valuable? How about:

As a therapist: 5 Strategies to Reduce Stress at the End of the Day

As an interior designer: Creating Stress-free Living Environment in Your Home

As a business consultant: Approaches Managers Can Use to Reduce Stress in the Workplace

As a professional tutor: How to Take the Stress Out of Your Child's Homework

As a financial planner: 4 Financial Vehicles to Put in Place So You Can Sleep at Night

Obviously, I could go on and on! But you get the idea. Based on your business or profession, you have knowledge, wisdom and insight that can serve people in so many ways. Use it to become known as the authority in your community.

Engage in Innovative Ways

There's a saying that says, "The more that you give, the more you receive." In Acts 20:35, the Bible refers to the fact that there is more happiness in giving than in receiving. I completely agree and always try to live my life like that. My goal is to give as much as I can, not because I'm going to get business in return. I know it will come. I do it because that's how the Universe works, right? What goes around comes around? Every action generates a reaction. That reaction may not be immediate, but it will certainly come.

So, we're going to keep our focus on giving value and doing it in a way that's *innovative*. I always say this and often use it in my signature line: "People before things. The more value you give, the more you'll receive."

> *"People before things. The more value you give, the more you'll receive."*

I was a third-grade teacher for six years and I talked really fast (and still do). My students would just sit there with their jaws dropping because I had so much energy. I had their complete attention because if they stopped looking even for a second, they wouldn't be able to keep up. They learned quickly how to follow along with me.

But I really got them engaged when I got innovative. For example, I love to cook, so every Friday I'd cook with the class. I'd relate cooking to life and whatever we were studying. If we were doing math and fractions, we'd make pizzas. I'd say, "Okay, let's cut the pizza in half. So, this is one half." Then I'd ask them, "Now how would you cut this pizza so that four people could eat it?" Instead of just showing fractions on the board, we cut up pizza. They got the concepts quickly and remembered them. Of course, making the pizza and eating it was fun, too!

This is adding value and being unique. I still see students from 20 years ago who tell me I was their favorite teacher ever. The point is that I was unique, cared immensely about them and was diligent in trying to be the best teacher I could be for them.

I also had them listen to musical theater. Honestly, at first most of them hated it. They were used to *Barney* or *Dora the Explorer* or *Beevis and Butthead*, and here I was playing *Phantom of the Opera*. Yet, because the music was so *different*, it caught their attention. They learned to love it, and they started asking me for more of it. When I see those kids now, they tell me, "I still love listening to *Phantom of the Opera*." That just makes me smile. Because I chose to be different, I made a difference twenty years ago to a bunch of eight-year-olds who still remember it to this day.

A lot of businesses or professionals send out information that is somewhat valuable, but it's *boring*. When I send out anything, I put it on steroids. In my real estate business, instead of just emailing a newsletter with tips for people wanting to sell their homes, I create a video on: "Hey, when you're selling your house, here's exactly what you should do!" The video is relatable and memorable, and I explain why they should do the things I recommend. I always show them the research behind it. For example, "If you fully stage your house, statistics show that you're going to make three to six percent more than if you don't."

I've also created a number of landing pages. A landing page is created to capture someone's contact information by giving something of value. Landing pages are super-simple to create, and you can find all sorts of templates online.

So how would you use it? For example, dance studio owner Nina Koch has a landing page with a brochure that tells parents all about having a child in a dance program: how much commitment it will take, how to make sure they have the right studio for their particular child, what they can expect in terms of cost for tuition, dance wear, etc. A financial planner could have a calculator that tells people how much they'll need to retire based on their goals. An architect could have reports on "Improvements with the Best Resale Value" or "Best Ideas for Kitchen Storage." Get the idea? It has to do with things you already know that a prospective client does not, and topics of interest to them.

Years ago, I ran into some software that you can put on your website to determine the value of a home. Using that software, I created a landing page of "What's your home worth?" At the time, no one had done it, so I got a ton of leads by providing potential sellers a good tool to find out the value of their home. After a while, agents in my area started copying me. Though I still use the calculator, I had to switch to something different.

I've made landing pages for first-time buyers, such as, "Know what you need to prepare to qualify for a mortgage" and "Five most common mistakes buyers make when purchasing a house." On these pages, I add in a mortgage calculator. For sellers, I've done pages like, "The seven most critical errors that sellers make that takes thousands of dollars from their bottom line." This page uses the home value calculator, but it first attracts potential sellers because they think, "Wow, I don't want to lose thousands of dollars. What should I make sure I don't do?"

If you are a small business consultant, you could do: Three Major Decisions Small Businesses Make That Will Cause Your Business to Go Bust. For a divorce attorney: Seven Deadly Sins of Divorce That Your Attorney Loves You to Make (aka More Dollars in Their Pocket). Or if you're training real estate agents: A Realtor's Biggest Pitfall: Assuming Everyone Will Remember Them. A professional tutor: How to Recognize Your Kid is Falling Behind *Before* They Fail.

For each landing page, the objective is to give people something of value. In exchange, you get their phone number and email address so you can market to them in the future, offering even more value. Once you have their information, you don't just let it go. You set them up in a marketing campaign, as we'll be discussing in Chapters Five and Six.

By continually being innovative, you're not only standing out from the crowd, which in itself is a huge benefit. You are also showing the community that you care, you work hard, and you are different.

Innovation is about creating fresh solutions for people in your community and presenting them in an interesting way. My third graders weren't necessarily crazy about math, but they all liked pizza! You are intelligent, you have ideas, you're creative, and you have a vision, right? That's all you need to be innovative.

> *Innovation is about creating fresh solutions for people in your community and presenting them in an interesting way.*

How you engage your community will probably look very different than what you're doing now, but it's going to work for you. Research what big businesses are doing. Go to content marketing websites and digital marketing websites. Implement and tweak what they are doing, and do it *early,* before anyone else in your community is doing it. Being an early adopter is key.

Think again about the examples I've shown you of the ways people and companies are using engagement marketing. What solutions, topics, or information would be timely and valuable to your community? Put those on a webinar, landing page, or (as I'll show you in Chapter Three) in a video.

Take the Next Step

1. *Next time you're online, take a moment to visit the website of one of the Big Guys I mentioned or some of the leaders in your business or profession. How do they position themselves? Do you feel like they are serving you or selling you? How could you apply this to your business?*

---

2. *Take a few minutes to think about your level of expertise in your industry. Where are you strong? How could you showcase your strengths? How could you improve in your weak areas?*

3. *Brainstorm 5 new ways you could engage your community. Be innovative and think outside of the box. As you brainstorm, don't critique yourself. Even really lame ideas can lead you to a great idea.*

For more information on becoming a Community Market Leader™ go to www.KristaMashore.com

CHAPTER THREE

GETTING YOURSELF OUT THERE

In the good old days, ambitious professionals would take their expertise out into the community by getting speaking engagements for local groups. They'd speak at their local Rotary Club, b2b forums, or Chamber of Commerce events. When email became popular, a lot of businesses and professionals started using email to blast out communications, specials or sales to their past network and maybe past clients.

That was then, and this is now. While it's still fine to do those things if you want (and if you do it *well*, thinking "serve, don't sell"), using the power of the internet *strategically* is going to get you much farther. And one of the most strategic ways to use the internet is with video.

Your Secret Weapon: Video

Statistically, on social media like Instagram and Facebook, videos get *12 times more* shares than text or photos! So, when you put your valuable information on video and post it, you get at least *12 times more people* viewing it! That's organic marketing that is free for you, right? And did you know when a website has video on it, people spend *88% more time* on that website? It seems pretty obvious that we should *all* be using video.

Video is hands down the most effective way to do engagement marketing. Even if you are a little bit shy, I encourage you to try it.

Something I always say is, "Be seen, be heard, be known." People need to know you in order for you to make an impact. Your job is to be an attention grabber so that you can stand out from all the noise.

> *People need to know you in order for you to make an impact.*

If you're not yet using video in your business, I encourage you to use it. As much as you might be afraid of the camera, as much as you might not feel comfortable at it, I am telling you that the discomfort is totally worth it. This practice alone—making informational videos— was a key factor in nearly doubling my gross commission from 2015 to 2016. It also was key in starting my coaching business. As time goes by and my businesses continue to grow, I attribute a lot of that growth to these videos.

According to research, 87% of online marketers use video in their digital marketing strategies. Marketers who use video grew 50% faster in revenue than those who didn't. Viewers retain 95% of a message when they watch it in

> *Marketers who use video grew 50% faster in revenue than those who didn't.*

a video, compared to only 10% when they read it in text. When people go online, they spend one third of their total online time watching videos. Also, 64% of customers say they're more likely to buy a product online after watching a video about it.

Video is the number one best thing that anyone can do to jumpstart their business. The number one thing in any business, no matter what it is, is video. Why? Because especially if *you* are your product (which, as a business or professional offering a service, you *are*), your job is to get people to know you, like you and trust you. Your job is to break down the barriers and any lack of trust or belief people have. Videos are the fastest, most effective way to do this.

Let me repeat myself: If a business owner (which you are, remember?) in *any* industry asked me what is the one single thing they can do to have the biggest and fastest impact on their business, I would tell them to start creating educational videos. The public doesn't know you from Adam and it's time to let them get to know you. You want them to see who and what you are all about. The more videos you distribute, the more you'll be remembered and perceived as the expert. Many people feel that attorneys, loan officers, insurance brokers, nail shops, ice cream shops and most other businesses and professionals are all the same. When looking for the service you offer, they don't think it makes any difference whether they use you, their neighbor who just opened a chiropractic office, their co-worker's wife who just got her real estate license, or their nephew who is three years out of law school.

It's your responsibility to show them that you are very different. When you expose the community to how different and knowledgeable you are, you start being seen as a person of authority. Today, I cannot go anywhere, and I mean *anywhere,* without someone telling me how much they love my videos. It might sound crazy, but my videos have definitely been the most impactful of just about anything I've done.

A video tells so much about who you are and how you run your business. You can show off without actually saying, "Hey, look how great I am!" You simply educate them about your process, the Who, What, and Why of every aspect of your business. Through your videos, you can show that not all psychotherapists, business consultants, or architects are the same, and that it *does* make a difference whether they choose you or their Cousin Bernie.

People typically make a judgement about you within a few seconds, so video gives them a chance to get to know your personality before they actually meet you in person. A study from Eric Wargo of the Association for Psychological Science titled, "How Many Seconds to a First Impression?" states that a first impression is actually formed in *milliseconds.*

People are often concerned that it takes too much time to create a video, but it is really the fastest way to get your market to know and trust you (and later in this chapter, I'll show you how to get lots of mileage out of each single video by "repurposing" it). With all of the noise and stuff out there, people are afraid and don't know really who they can trust or who they can believe in. The more you use video, so your audience gets to see you, the more that you become a real person to them. They start to feel they know you because they see you so often on your videos. Once you start doing it and get familiar with making videos, it takes hardly any time at all. I can create a video now in less time than it takes to write an email or make a phone call!

Okay, I know that some of you are slamming on the brakes right now. "Nope. Never gonna happen. I am NOT going to get in front of a camera then show it to a bunch of people I've never met!" I get it. I felt the same way and many of my students felt the same way. In fact, Julee Patterson of Gateway Properties in Auburn, California absolutely *refused* to do this part of the program at first. She was nervous and embarrassed and worried about what people would think of her. We finally got her to try it and now she's become a video maven. She's become a super star in her community and her business is booming. If you go on YouTube, you can see all of the great, creative videos she's produced. In fact, she's so good at it now that she was invited to present at a video master mind conference in Florida. And this is someone who started out terrified of video!

To make it easier to record your videos, you can set a day aside each week where you record maybe eight content videos for the month, or four videos for the next two weeks. Schedule a specific time slot when you won't get interrupted. Get the room set up and be all ready to go with ideas of what you're going to say. Then for each video, just change your clothes and maybe change your hairstyle so you look a little different. Recording multiple videos at one time is much less overwhelming.

With videos, shorter is better. Keep them under 30 seconds if you can and give as much value as possible within that timeframe. Don't start by saying your name or introducing yourself. Start it with something really catchy. You have only 6 seconds to capture their attention so don't waste that time by saying your name. Make it count and hook them in immediately. For example, a tax account-ant might say, "I've got three huge tips that are going to save you a bundle of money at tax time." A landscape designer might lead with, "I've got four easy ways you can drought-proof your landscape." After the catchy opening, you can say your name.

You want to let them know what they're going to learn and why they should listen. Your basic video outline can be:

1. Catch their attention and let them know what you're going to provide them, then state your name.
2. Identify with their pain or issue.
3. Without bragging, state why you are the authority figure and why they should listen to you. (For example, "I've helped hundreds of couples navigate wedding planning and actually enjoy the process while getting the wedding they've always wanted.")
4. Give them the solutions and tips that will help them

A few years ago, people said that a three-minute video was good. All the research now shows 30 seconds or less is better. By the time this book is written, it might change again. A study I just read stated that one minute of video is equivalent to 1.8 million words (which kinda makes me wonder why I keep writing books!). Studies show that 20% of people will leave after the first 10 seconds of watching a video. So, you need to make sure that you're engaging and motivating them to continue watching.

If you can't cover everything you want to cover in 30-45 seconds, make a couple of videos as Parts 1 and 2, or even 3 and 4. People are in a hurry and won't pay attention for much longer than a minute. You want viewers to be able to watch your video in-between other things they do (i.e., while waiting in line for their Starbucks). As you get comfortable, you may want to create charts or graphs to illustrate what you're sharing and add visual interest.

An important note: 80% of all videos are watched *without* sound. So, it's good to have the words show up on the bottom of the video if you can. Get your video transcribed and put them on your videos. Trint.com will do your transcription for about $15 per hour and Rev. com will give you a transcription for $1 per minute. (The difference is that Rev.com is a real person doing the transcribing but Trint.com is based on software, so you need a pretty clear recording to use Trint.com to get a good transcription.)

"Video mirroring" means copying somebody else's video style that is working. Find someone either in or outside of your business or profession who is already well known and who is attracting followers and customers. Watch their videos and webinars. Read their content. Study them. Notice what's working. If it's working for them, it can work for you.

You can even have a video you particularly like transcribed and learn the language of successful people in your field. Listen to the questions, feedback, and remarks they get. Make these people your personal mentors. I'm not saying to copy their material literally. That wouldn't be ethical. Simply learn from them, then create your own material. Don't reinvent the wheel. Follow in the footsteps of those who have figured it out then add your own personality, your own approach, and knowledge. If you can't find someone in your field, find videos in other similar fields. Notice what you like and don't like. Notice what attracts you and what you can emulate.

One of the biggest hurdles people have is the fear of the video process itself. They worry about having just the right equipment and set up. I tell people who are starting out that you just need to *do* it. In the very beginning, I would encourage you to set a goal and create a video every day. Send it to your friend, or send it to your mom, or send it to your spouse. Just ask them to watch it and critique you. No one is perfect, and no one expects you to be perfect. If you don't just start, you never will. You've just got to put one foot in front of the other and do it. Actually, I've learned that people prefer you to not be perfect. So, go ahead and be perfectly imperfect. Just go for it!

Don't worry about the lighting or getting a tripod or how your make-up looks or having the perfect backdrop. All of those are just excuses, right? Everybody has a cell phone or laptop. Right now, just use your cell phone. Pick it up, push record, make sure you've got decent light, and go for it. Your goal with these first videos is to just get comfortable doing it. No one will see them (except people who have seen you a million times). By watching your own videos, you'll see what you need to improve on.

In my program, I teach people to do 10 video text messages a day to past clients, to their sphere of influence folks, or even to people they met at a game, party or at the store. One great strategy is to look that person up on their social media and find something great they've recently experienced, like having a baby, kid graduating from school, cool life event, etc. Just say "Hey I was thinking of you and wanted to reach out and congratulate you on little Johnny going to preschool." Don't ask for business, don't ask for referrals, just show interest. Do this and you'll be amazed at how just this one thing can truly change your business.

Whenever you do a video, record for a few seconds, stop and then check it out. Make sure the lighting is okay, so you don't have some crazy glare. Make sure you can actually see yourself. (Yes, I've recorded a whole video where the camera was turned off or my phone was filming my feet!) Make sure that the background is appropriate (I made a video at home once then discovered my undies were drying in the background!) and you can hear yourself clearly (no dogs barking or wind howling). If everything checks out, just go ahead and record your video. You can do a couple of takes but do NOT try to be perfect! Imperfect is much more engaging and relatable. It's okay to be *perfectly imperfect.* Just start and do it!

> *Imperfect is much more engaging and relatable. It's okay to be perfectly imperfect.*

You don't need expert lighting or an Oscar-worthy script. You just need to take good information and present it in a way that is valuable and meaningful to people.

Even after the hundreds of videos I've done, am I perfect? No. Do I make mistakes and stumble over words? Yes, all the time. Do I care? No! I'm human, right? And, the people in my community don't care either. They want me, and they want *you*, to be human. In fact, I'll often post my bloopers. People love seeing them and it shows that I'm not a robot or perfect.

These days, when I do a video, I don't practice at all. But starting out, you may want to do a couple of run-throughs until you find your rhythm. If you feel self-conscious, take your focus off yourself. Focus instead on the people you're making this video for: What do they need to know? How can you explain it in a way they'll understand? How can you help them? How can you add value to them, provide service to them? Pretend you're talking to just one person, not a stadium full of people.

You may want to make some notes, so you stay on track, and a brief list of talking points that you want to cover. Then, don't stress—just go out there and do it! If you do enough research and know your topic, you'll speak with confidence, and that's how you start to be recognized as an authority in your area.

I have always had a super fear of public speaking. My coach gave me some great advice: "Krista, don't make it about you. Make it about how you're helping people, and what they are going to get from your speaking. Think about how you are helping them, and how you can change their lives for the better." This alone has helped me to step out of my shell and turn my nervousness into excitement.

In her book, *The 5 Second Rule,* Mel Robbins writes about courage. She says that anytime you are nervous or have anxiety about anything, tell yourself that those nerves are truly excitement. Talk yourself out of nervousness and into excitement. It truly works!

Let me just warn you about something: When you're an expert in something, it's easy to forget what you *didn't know* when you first started. In other words, make sure that you're presenting your information in ways that people without your expertise can understand. In writing my books and putting together my training courses, I've continually had to remind myself of that. I know what it takes to be a Community Market Leader™ backwards and forwards. When I started teaching it, I had to take fifteen steps back and start from the very beginning. I had to get a lot more specific about each piece and not just gloss over a technique or concept as if everybody already understood what I meant. (If they did, why would they bother learning from me?)

When I'm teaching my students about digital marketing, social media and funnels, I realize that this is new to them. I start with the strategy and work my way down to more detail. I try to make things as easy to understand as when I was teaching third grade. When I'm educating buyers and sellers about the real estate process, I take each and every aspect and break it down in layman's terms. We assume everyone knows how the real estate process works. Yet, the majority of people have no clue. They're nervous and they need it to be broken down.

I do the same in my informational videos. When people see how I break concepts down on the videos, they're more comfortable with me. They know that I know what I'm doing and I'm taking the time to walk them through it. Keep this in mind. People are smart, but they don't know everything that you know, and they don't know your lingo. Explain whatever it is in a way that a non-expert could get it. Keep it simple and in laymen's terms. Think about it: How often do people need most professional services? They usually only need a tax accountant once per year, a mortgage every four or five years at the most, and hopefully, they'll only need a divorce mediator once in their lifetime if ever! So, they probably won't remember the process and they don't know what to expect. So keep it simple.

In my inner circle (which is like a master mind group), we've been taught to do a three-part training video series with each video being about five minutes long. In this series, you start with the basics of whatever industry you do as it applies to the client. It's really all of the things you may be saying when you first meet them to explain how the process is going to work and what you will do for them. New clients are given these videos to watch *prior* to meeting with you. When you actually meet, you may repeat some of the information for emphasis, but mostly, you'll just be answering any questions they have. There are several benefits to this: First of all, the client already feels like they know and trust you and they are prepared with questions when you meet. Also, they have these videos and can refer back to them in case they get confused. An added bonus is that it can save you a heck of a lot of time! You don't have to review basics with each and every client that comes in, but you can get right to work with them. This approach works for any industry.

Before I knew about this, I had a similar idea. A couple of years ago, I recorded my listing presentation, totally spur of the moment and with no practice. I asked a colleague to act as a potential seller.

Now I send that video before I go to a listing appointment. It saves me time and, more importantly, establishes me as the agent of choice. My closing ratio was around 97% for listings and I rarely had to reduce commission on my side. Why? The clients see the value in what I provide. Provide enough value and *show* the value you provide. If you do this, you will be unbeatable.

In my coaching business, before clients even get on the phone with one of my salespeople, the client has already watched targeted videos that explain who I am and how I can help them. Every once in a while, someone will get on the phone with us and they haven't seen my videos prior to the call. The odds of that person converting into a client are really slim compared to those who have had prior exposure.

Don't use any of your videos to say, "Call me to handle your mortgage" or "Call my office if you have back pain." Instead begin with, "Here's something you might need help with or might want to know." Then close with, "Please let me know what other videos I can do to help you. I'm here to help." Don't be asking for the sale by saying, "I'm great! Hire me!" Before you ever get to that point, you should give them a ton of value. Do that well and you won't even have to ask for the sale.

As Glenn Hoffman of Discovery Bay Insurance Services points out, when you're in the professional services business, you're in a "pull through" business. "Soda is a push through business. You stick a dollar in a vending machine and out comes your Coke. But in a professional service, like my insurance business, we're a 'pull through' business. I need to pull clients through the process by always being of service, letting them get to know me and showing them that they can trust me."

One of the huge benefits of sharing your expertise through video is just that—people get familiar with you and you don't feel like a stranger. When my clients enter our coaching and training programs, it's like they already know me. Even if I've never met them before, I've developed trust and a relationship with them through all the videos they've seen of me giving good information. I don't have to "sell myself" to them. I'm already sold.

To get to that point, you need to make sure that your informational videos show up *everywhere*. (For more insight and information on videos, go to http://www.theultimatemarketingplaybook. com/member.)

Being Everywhere

Now, what do you do with those videos once you've started making them? You distribute them strategically!

Here are some statistics to consider: Cisco says that global internet traffic in 2020 will be 95 times more than the volume in 2005. Internet traffic will average 21 GB per person by 2020 versus 7 GB per capita in 2015. Google Analytics Hour of Day Report states, "Most websites receive the majority of their visits during the day when people are awake and have predictably busy periods during weekdays. You may see spikes in website traffic just before school or work time in the morning (7am to 9 am), or at lunchtime (12 pm to 2 pm), or right after school or work (4 pm to 6 pm)." Knowing this gives you a good clue about when you should be sending emails out!

The key is to use the power of the internet and post your videos in as many places as you can to get the most exposure. Of course, you'll post them on your website and email them to your client and prospect lists (paying attention to the times most people go online per Google Analytics). You also want to post them on Facebook, Instagram, LinkedIn, Twitter, and any new social media platform that comes along. I'm sure that by the time this book is published—and maybe before I finish this sentence!—someone will create the new *new* of social media platforms. You and I will be on that too.

> *The key is to use the power of the internet and post your videos in as many places as you can to get the most exposure.*

For example, we have a YouTube channel for Krista Mashore Coaching. As I'm writing this, we just launched it. Within a month's time we had *10,000 hours* of people watching us, on our YouTube channel. On our Facebook ads for Homes by Krista, we know that people watch 167 hours to 555 hours (and climbing) of each video within 14 days. Plus, these videos spread organically because they don't just run while we're running ads. We also have them on You-Tube. Now imagine this, how many open houses would I have to do to get 555 hours of people listening and watching me? Think about how much exposure and branding that is to my company and I. How many presentations at Rotary meetings would you have to give to get that kind of exposure in one month?

When using the internet, the most important rule of thumb is to **show up where your target market is**. If you advertised on TV, you would choose the network and shows that your target market watches, right? Your ads targeted to kids might show up on Nickelodeon but if your target is young men, you might go for ESPN. You'd refine it further by picking specific shows, for example, the *Ellen Degeneres Show* is a favorite among women who are 25 to 54.

No, I'm *not* recommending that you market on television! Marketing through the internet is way more cost effective. With all the new technologies out there, you can get your message to thousands of people in your community almost instantly. Even so, you still want to focus on using the correct platform(s) for the target market you've identified.

It's really important that you pick a platform wisely, then master that platform and do it relentlessly. You want people to get familiar with you and count on your showing up on that platform before you expand to other platforms. If you try to do all of them or even a few of them, you won't be effective on any of them. (For more information on specific social media platforms, click http://www.theultimatemarketingplaybook.com/member to download a free report.)

For my real estate business, I complete a new educational or market update video several times a week. I've found the sweet spot to be about three videos per week, but that could change, so continue to educate yourself. For my coaching and training business I create videos continually and distribute them to my audience on multiple platforms. We will take clips from one video and distribute it on another channel. All videos are distributed on numerous digital platforms. I also use search engine optimization (SEO), which we will get into in Chapter Five.

Everywhere I go in my community, people come up to me saying, "Hi, Krista!" Half the time, I have no idea who they are. They feel like they know me because they see me on social media and other marketing vehicles constantly. I act as if I know them, too. But when my husband, Steve, asks, "Who is that?"' I have to confess that I have absolutely no idea (if you're local and reading this, I still love you lol). By showing up in videos, you become a celebrity in your area for your business or profession. You literally become a rock star, you attract business!

I was getting my hair done the other day, and my hairdresser said, "The lady over there kept saying she knew you from somewhere." Apparently, the woman finally figured it out and told my hairdresser, "I know where I've seen her. I see her all over Facebook. I love her videos!" The woman lived in a town about 45 minutes away. I stopped by and talked to her and she said her family discusses the videos. She was really happy to meet me and said she felt like she already knew me. I am not exaggerating when I say that I literally have hundreds of stories like this.

Human connection is the key to personal and career success. I might never have run into that woman. Yet, through my videos, she had connected with me on a personal level. That's a part of the definition of engagement marketing: marketing that involves the creation and sharing of online material (such as videos, blogs, and social media posts) that does not explicitly promote a brand or a business but is intended to stimulate interest and connection with its products or services.

I've used this same exact strategy to launch my coaching business. Even though my coaching business is on a national not local level, I've still been able to make that human connection through video. I created tons of free video content about keys to success which established me as an authority. My first book also contributed. I made sure that the book was well-written, had valuable content and was very professional-looking. Then people from all over actually saw, "Wow, she's a best-selling published author and she really knows what she's talking about."

Now, anytime I go to a conference, whether it's in Florida or in Dallas, I have people stopping me and wanting to take pictures with me. They tell me how much they love my book, and they love my videos and how inspiring I've been. Remember, the point is to give value and establish yourself as an authority, not just become a celebrity (and trust me, I'm no celebrity, lol). Lately, we've really focused heavily on YouTube and Instagram. Within one month, we had over 10,000 hours of video views just on YouTube. Then we launched a podcast called *F.I.R.E.D Up with Krista Mashore* and had 21,500 downloads and just over 200 five-star reviews, all in just ten weeks. See how amazing it can be? (To hear the podcast, go to https://fire.kristamashore.com/podcast.)

Now, if you're thinking that you can send out your information with a well-written email blast and get the same result, you can't. Think about your own experience: Compare learning by reading an instructive email versus watching a video class online. Which one makes you feel most connected with the teacher?

Plus, statistics on open rates for email shows that it's declining. Here are a couple of graphs from Google analytics:

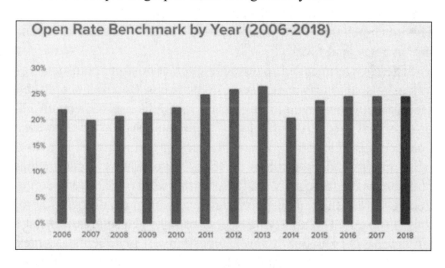

	Open Rate	Click-through Rate
Benelux	16%	20%
Denmark	31%	23%
Germany	25%	24%
Norway	18%	10%
Sweden	17%	12%
Switzerland	29%	18%
United Kingdom	13%	13%
Rest of the world	40%	5%

When you use email, your email has to be absolutely irresistible for people to open it. One of the ways to make it irresistible is by creating a short video for whatever you want to communicate.

I was recently at the airport heading to a master mind group with one of my high-level digital marketing coaches. I was in the restroom getting ready and I lost track of time. All of the sudden I was running to the runway as they were calling my name saying, "Last call." When I got to the door, the flight attendant asked me, "Are you Krista Mashore? *The* Krista Mashore?" I said, "Yes, that's me. About to miss my plane." Recently at a Ylopo conference in Los Angeles, I had numerous people come up to me and say how much they love my content. It's not just local. It's happening on a national level.

There's a term called "parasocial interactions" or "parasocial relationships" that was coined back in the fifties. It means people can feel like they know you through mass media like seeing you on TV or on social media. Even before TV, people used to feel like they knew certain celebrities, political figures or sports heroes based on what they'd read about them. In today's world with social media, you don't have to be a TV star to have that kind of effect on people. People stare at their phones for hours every day and, if you're there, they'll see you. I'm not trying to brag or say, "I'm so great." What I am emphasizing is that it's *working*. Many of my clients say they have many Realtor® friends. Many of my coaching clients have heard about dozens of coaches. But they chose to call me because I am so knowledgeable, innovative, and different!

Keep in mind that many people who will seek professional services typically start thinking and research it ahead of time. If they're buying a home or arranging for a mortgage, they statistically start 4-6 months *prior* to pulling the trigger. Someone who realizes they should have a financial plan probably spends a few months thinking about it first. A couple in trouble may not be quite ready to divorce but they probably are getting curious about it. Someone with back pain is undoubtedly looking into options before deciding what to do or where to go.

These people will research and gather information prior to making their choice. Help them choose you by standing out and giving them the information they need to make an educated decision about the services they need.

I've used the exact same strategies for my coaching and training business that I used in growing my real estate business. I read and studied and went to lots of seminars to become an expert in the field. Then I made tons of free video content and got my name out there using social media and the internet. I also wrote and marketed my first book. The book was my segue into coaching because people actually saw, "Wow, she's an authority figure!" BTW, if you decide to write a book, please don't think you can just spit out a few pages and slap a fancy cover on it. As in everything you do, you have to give real value and offer a high-quality product.

Attorney Carol Delzer of Family Law Center took the time to write a really great book, *Divorce Done Easier*. The book doesn't just talk about divorce law, it focuses on many of the emotional, financial, and life-changing aspects of a divorce. She sells the book on Amazon, but she also uses it in a number of other ways. "I always give it as a thank-you for a referral. I have distributed the book to therapists in the area because it covers so many issues their clients might be facing. I even have free copies that I give away to anyone who comes to my office (so feel free to stop by!). The point is that, whether they use my divorce mediation services or choose another route, I've given them something that will be valuable for anyone facing this situation. And they'll remember me for that value."

Let me just tell you that writing a book—a *good* book—takes a lot of time and energy and it can be expensive to publish. If it's something that you really want to do, do it! Just keep in mind, you need valuable content (and don't worry about giving away your precious secrets!) tailored for your target market, quality writing (get a good editor), and a professional looking cover (you can find graphic artists online). I prefer to have my books in print, but to save costs of printing and shipping, you can make yours into an eBook that people download.

We all have to really come from a perspective of value. It's sometimes scary, but in many businesses and professional services, much of the competition is online now in everything from healthcare to mortgages to online bankruptcy services. Yikes! You know they can't provide the service you provide and people using online services get what they pay for, but many people won't understand the difference.

If someone approaches you and says they want to use some service online rather than your service, I wouldn't argue with them. I'd be helpful and tell them some of the pitfalls to watch out for and how to make sure they get what they need. Then just let them go.

Because here is the important thing: You don't want leads, you want *clients*. Quit worrying about landing every single lead. You don't need them. Don't chase them. If you focus on the full sales cycle (Chapters Five through Eight), you'll end up with clients, often lifelong clients.

It's All Recyclable!

Any great content you produce, whether written, audio, or video, can and should be repurposed! Repurposing just means using what you've got in different ways and in different formats. For example, after you create a terrific video, you can have that video transcribed (via something like Rev.com or Trint.com) Then you just clean up the transcription and bingo! You've got a blog. If you posted the video on Instagram, you might post the blog on your website or as an article on your business' Facebook group. And if you posted the video on your social media platform, you can schedule it to be posted again a few months down the line or sent out to your email list.

You can take that video and put it onto YouTube. You can take the sound from the video and use just the audio as a podcast or sound clips on social media. From just one video you, get 8 different ways to repurpose it: 1) Record the video and place on Facebook as a video. 2). Get it transcribed and put the transcription as a long form post on Facebook (be sure to add emoji's and put them at the end of the sentences so it doesn't interrupt reading). 3) Place the video on your website and 4) place the transcription on your website. Google *loves* video. Your website content helps you with SEO (search engine optimization). 5) Place the video on YouTube, then 6) put it on Instagram. 7) Make the audio version into a podcast, and 8) take sentences that are especially impactful out of the videos and use them as "quote cards". (To make a quote card, you just put some graphics around a great quote, include your name as the person who said it, and post it everywhere!)

This is video repurposing. When people tell me they don't have time to do a video, I show them this strategy and they realize they can't afford NOT to find the time to do it!

If you've written a book, you can take a chapter or part of a chapter and use it as a script for a video or as a blog. You can create a free webinar out of one of the chapters or create a series of mini books using different sections. Whenever you create great content in any form, get creative about how you can repurpose it to get the most out of your efforts.

Does This Really Work?

Now, if you're new to your industry, you're probably thinking, "Oh my gosh! I'm brand new. How can I do this? I'm not an expert." Well, as soon as you start giving information, value, advice, and tips, you become the authority, even if you're brand new. You might have less experience than somebody else, but if you're the one out there talking about it, being top of mind awareness, showing up in front of people, giving them advice, giving them value, you're the authority. You're the authority more than the person who has 10 or 15 years of experience because the community you're trying to reach doesn't know about that person.

I've got so many case studies of people who are relatively new who, once they followed this strategy, did phenomenally well. Alex Mayer had been in the real estate business for just two years. Now, he's closing a significant amount of business and, since he's been in our program, he says his referral business has gone up four times. He's a new agent compared to many others, but because people are seeing him everywhere, they see him as the authority figure. They trust him and, of course, he does the best possible job for them once they are clients. Two of my other coaching clients, Tara and Lakota, have been in their business for less than two years. Their business has increased by 500% in sales and 600% in units in less than a year. A brand-new agent, Sue LeFavri is taking my course and she was just nominated by her town as "The Best Realtor." Here's the crazy thing: Sue has not done a lot of real estate yet. Still, she's recognized as an authority because she's been producing video content that informs and educates her community, so she's become the Community Market Leader.

We've got hundreds of people of all different shapes and sizes, young and old who have done really well following the engagement marketing model. We've got people who are brand new in their industry who are doing amazing. We've got people who have been in their industry and are already top producers who have increased their business significantly.

So, yes, it does work. And if you're an experienced loan officer, attorney, architect or any other type of professional, and you're willing to do what it takes to become an *authority* in what you do, it will definitely work for you too.

CHAPTER FOUR

YOUR BUSINESS: ONE OF A KIND, NOT ONE OF THE PACK

I want to clear up a huge misunderstanding that many businesses or professionals have who are in the services industry. Even if you work for a larger company, in most cases, you are *not* an employee. You're a business owner. You usually need to develop your own clients. You are an entrepreneur. And because you're an entrepreneur, you need to stand out from the pack, not just do what folks around you are doing.

For example, many new loan officers try to "fit in" and follow in the footsteps of mortgage professionals around them. They act as if they've been given a job description with certain duties: go to real estate networking events, cold call real estate firms, work with anyone who walks through the door, work weekends and nights, and answer their cell phone 24/7. To be successful, they assume they can't choose what hours to work. The "job" drives their schedule. They don't think they can choose what clients to have or what their business looks like. With just a few variations, service professionals in other industries could tell the exact same story. They've been given outdated, inaccurate notions about what it really takes to be successful.

I get it. When I started in real estate, I did all the things I saw others doing. Broke and newly single, I even knocked on doors looking for leads, which took hours and hours away from my two little girls. But I was extremely motivated (to be more accurate, I was desperate!).

I didn't know it at the time, but the Universe (call it God, a higher power, whatever) had something bigger in store for me. When I left my teaching career abruptly to dive into a new career, it felt very daring and scary. The crazy part about this story is that if I hadn't taken that leap of faith, if I had let my fear of change get in my way, I would be in an incredibly different place today. Looking back, I'm so glad that when I had the inclination to change careers and dive in, I did it! Remember, my goal was to be a "stay at home mom" but my plans quickly changed when my husband left.

Because of my success today, people seem to think that it's all been smooth sailing. It hasn't. And, I didn't get to where I am just because I'm bubbly and smart—honestly, I've heard people say that! The reason I've been in the Top 1% in real estate and the reason I've had such great success already in my coaching and training business is because I have an incredible work ethic, drive for excellence, strong appetite for educating myself, and I'm different. I've always approached this career as a serious business owner, even in the beginning when I was frightened and insecure. I always put people before things and love serving those who trust me to help them.

You've got to start thinking like an entrepreneur, a business owner.

> *You've got to start thinking like an entrepreneur, a business owner.*

It's true that you don't have quite as many choices when you're first starting. When I began in real estate, I focused on buyers and did a lot of the traditional things like open houses to get leads. But even back then, I was thinking like an entrepreneur, not an employee. I tried to do things a little differently than people in my office. I analyzed what was working and what wasn't. I knew that I was the one who had to create the kind of business and success I wanted. I constantly took classes to learn. I tried different things and failed, then failed again.

Don't get me wrong. My results were outstanding in my first year. But I wasn't as innovative then as I am now. I worked like crazy, but I was timid about standing out and making myself known. I wish I had understood the awesome power of being bold and innovative. You don't have to make that same mistake. Whatever your business or profession, jump into your business *boldly*. Make a difference and be different. Create your unique business and do the things your colleagues and competitors are not doing. Be an entrepreneur.

> *Whatever your business or profession, jump into your business boldly. Make a difference and be different.*

Hire a coach. This may seem crazy to you, but as successful as I am, I continue to have a coach. I'll talk about this again in Chapter Eleven. But, for now, just know that it is difficult to do something new and be the best of the best on your own. You may need mentoring, constant pushing and help at implementing all you need to do to be the best, to stand out, and to make it happen! Don't be a lemming. Don't just follow the leader. Be the leader!!

My goal was always to be #1 in the market. In the beginning in real estate, I'd study the super successful brokers and figure out what I could do to be as successful as they were. I kept the techniques or approaches that fit me and discarded the rest. I started studying other businesses outside of real estate to see what made them successful. Then, I took what I learned and applied it to my business. For example, early on, I realized that I wanted more control over my time, which meant dealing with sellers rather than buyers. So, I turned my attention toward making that happen.

The point is that I didn't just drift along "doing real estate" and you don't just want to drift along "doing landscape designs" or "doing yoga classes." Create your vision—which might change from time to time—of the type of business you really want. Then focus on putting that business together.

Your goal may not be to become #1 in your industry. You may just want more revenue stability or to work with a different type of client. You may want a business that secures your financial freedom, or one that lets you control your time more. Whatever it is, the principles I'm sharing will help you get there. **But you need to start with your unique vision of what kind of business you want, then design your brand around that.**

As a service business or professional, who you are—your expertise, your personality, your character, your work ethic, your connections, and your approach—*is* your business. To build a really successful business that will also make your life more fulfilling, that business has to be a reflection of who you authentically are. A lot of new professionals might try to build a business that looks like the hot shot guy or gal sitting next to them. But that's a mistake. You want to discover the specific, unique value only you can bring to the table. Then you want to incorporate that value into your brand. To get started, get specific about who you are and who you want to work with.

Develop Your Niche

Have you heard the phrase, "Niches make riches?" It's true. In professional services in just about any industry, if you put yourself out there as a generalist, you've got a ton of competition. As a generalist, you have to spread your marketing efforts and budget really thin to expose all the possible services you could offer and capture all categories of clients out there. You might think that by creating a niche, you will be losing too many opportunities. You won't. By doing a good job in your niche, you will end up capturing business that is outside of it. On the other hand, if you try to relate to everybody, you won't capture anybody.

When I wrote my first book aimed at Realtors®, my editor kept reminding me that if I try to write a book for *everybody*, it won't be very useful. The raw beginners won't understand it, it will be too simple for very experienced readers, and real estate hobbyists will think it's too much effort. By honing my message down to a specific type of real estate agent—someone who really wanted to get the most out of their real estate business—I could give clear and valuable information. When I wrote my second book, I honed in on people who wanted to stop being employees or who were newly retired and who wanted to become entrepreneurs. This book is geared to local businesses and professionals in the service industry. Even though many of my strategies would work for things like retail or direct sales, the issues and challenges of local businesses and professionals who provide a service are different. So, the examples and illustrations I use are targeted to that niche.

Creating a niche is also going to save you thousands of dollars in marketing. You won't keep throwing away marketing dollars trying to attract everyone. Instead, you'll focus your efforts and money on attracting the client that you want to work with. If your focus is millennials and first-time home buyers, you won't waste money on an ad in AARP or posters in a senior housing community. You'll focus on text messaging, social media, and apps like Twitter, Instagram, Pinterest, Tik Tok, and Snapchat. If you're focused on yoga classes for older people, you won't rely solely on text blasts or mobile phone-compatible landing pages or social media sites. You'll use snail mail and email, even hand deliver flyers to seniors' community centers or advertise in their monthly newsletter. When you narrow in on who your perfect client is, you know exactly who to market to, how to market, whether it's on blogs, social media, any of your landing pages, your lead pages— whatever you're doing, you know who you're focusing on.

Have you ever watched an ad on TV and had absolutely no idea what the ad was about? That's because you are not the person the ad is trying to attract, and the advertiser doesn't care if you get it. They've designed that ad to hit home with the specific market who does understand it.

Remember, you don't have to make an impact on the entire world. You just have to reach a few. Let's put this into perspective. If, as an architect, you had three clients a month last year, and your goal is five per month this year, that's only twenty-four more clients that you need to reach this year. It's not a million. If your goal is to fill one more dance class of twenty students, that's just twenty more families you need to find. If your goal is to close fifty more loans than you did last year, that's fifty clients or about four per month you need to attract. Who do you want those new clients or students to be?

I encourage my students to come up with their "client avatars" who are representations of your perfect client. I learned about this from one of my mentors, Russell Brunson, and many other highly successful marketers teach it as well. You may already be thinking about the people you want to work with. By creating some avatars, you begin to understand what makes them tick. For example, when I started my coaching business, I wrote down that I wanted to work with people who are go-givers, who love learning, who are high achievers, who want to serve people and who want to be at the top of their game. Then I thought about people I already know who are like that and asked myself: Where do they get their information? Where do they shop? What do they enjoy doing? What do they read? What issues or challenges do they face? What is most important to them? What are their priorities? What are their hobbies? What stage of life are they in? Who do they follow on social media? How old are they? Are they married or single?

One of the most important questions you can ask to help define your avatar is, "What keeps them up at night?" In other words, what worries them? What upsets them? What do they have in their lives that causes them pain of some kind? What are they afraid of? People are drawn to things they love but they are even more motivated to get away from things that are painful in some way. To connect with them, you need to let them know that you really understand their pain points as well as their desires. In fact, all of your marketing messages will be tailored around those two ends of the spectrum.

As I started my coaching and training business, I targeted professionals in real estate or in real estate-related fields. Why? Because this is where I had the most familiarity, credibility and connections. As that business grew, I expanded to other local businesses and service professionals. Why? Because many business owners and service professionals are out on their own and not employees, so they would recognize the value in what I offer. Also, they are most likely to be able to afford my training and coaching services. Even though my strategies could help just about anyone succeed, they aren't my niche. If I attract people outside this niche (which I do), great. But I tailor my message and marketing to my avatars, my niche.

If you're having trouble finding your client avatar, go back to your past clients—the good ones, *not* the ones you wish you'd never met—and interview them. "Why did you choose me? What qualities did you like about me?"

While you're at it, ask them how you could have improved in your services and relationship with them. Let them know you are open to constructive criticism. Don't be afraid to do this. You'll learn something new about yourself and your ideal client. If you hear a complaint from one person who has the courage to speak out, you probably have other clients who were unhappy. The White House Office of Consumer Affairs claims that for every customer who bothers to complain, **26** other customers remain silent.

While you're doing this, think about your good clients and what attributes they share in common. Maybe they are all smart or really diligent in doing whatever they needed to do. Maybe they are active in the community or have tight-knit families.

What are your past clients' interests? What are their desires? What do they want? If you aren't sure, ask them. What are they looking for in life? What makes them tick? Develop your client avatar with this information in mind.

At the beginning of this chapter, we talked about starting with who you are and who you want your target market to be. If you work with people who are at odds with you, the whole process of delivering your service will be much more difficult. Personally, I don't want to fight with my clients in a tug of war over dominance. I want my clients to trust me and know that I have their best interests at heart. Learn to say "no" to clients that aren't a fit so you can focus on the clients you want (We truly have a strong No A-Hole Policy in my company, you should too). If you go to http://www.theultimatemarketingplaybook.com/member, you'll find an example Client Avatar Worksheet. Use that worksheet to create the perfect client avatar for yourself.

> *Learn to say "no" to clients that aren't a fit so you can focus on the clients you want*

For example, attorney Carol Delzer knows that she likes to work with couples who have been to couples' counseling before coming to see her. "They've already talked through some of their issues and they're clear that divorce is the option they want. They are 'consciously uncoupling' by that point. They each have some self-awareness and usually have gotten through some of that first anger and hurt. With this, we're able to get to good compromises and creative solutions much more quickly." Will she work with couples who haven't been in counseling? Sure. But she targets her dream clients.

Debbi Galvan, a senior loan officer with Land Home Financial Services has had a long career and now focuses on "boomerang buyers," people who have lost their homes in the recent recession and are now trying to get back into a home. These people aren't going online to get their loans. They'll need a little more help to qualify, and after 19 years in the business, Debbi knows she can help them. When she was coming up with her avatar of who she wanted to work with, she said, "I really started thinking about who are the people that need help and once I could give them that help, I'd know they wouldn't leave me no matter what." The work is satisfying to her and she gets a ton of referrals from her clients.

When Nina Koch opened her dance studio, East County Preforming Arts Center, she was most interested in all that dance instruction has to offer that goes beyond dance skills. "While other schools might emphasize developing competitive or professional dance skills, in our classes, we emphasize the whole child, not just making them into great dancers. We want their experience with us to build their self-esteem, their self-confidence, and to help them develop discipline and a good work ethic. We want each child to feel good about themselves, no matter what their skill level."

In his insurance business over the past several years, Glenn Hoffman nurtured an interesting niche: the tow truck industry. "I had twenty years of experience with clients in the building industry. Then I started focusing on auto repair shops, auto body shops, and dealerships. As a young man, I was an automotive technician, a blue-collar guy who worked in an auto repair shop. I understand what those businesses face and what they need from insurance. I can talk their language. That led me to my third niche, transportation and tow truck clients." Though he handles all kinds of clients, Glenn has been especially successful with what he calls all of his "tool belt" clients. "When you see those yellow AAA tow trucks driving by, a lot of them are insured by my company."

When you decide the kind of business you want, *everything* should reflect that niche, even the way you dress! If you're business consultant who specializes in large corporate organizations, you probably don't want to show up to your first meeting in khakis and a golf shirt. On the flip side, if you're consulting with small Mom and Pop businesses, that three-piece suit might be too much. I know a Realtor™ not too far from me who sells ranch properties. She wears jeans and boots to her listing appointments. In meeting my clients with high end homes, that outfit would never fly! By what she wears, the woman who sells ranch property is saying, "I'm one of you. I know what a working ranch is and how it works. I know how to market your property." When I show up in heels and a business suit, I'm saying, "I'm a professional and I know what I'm doing. I'm comfortable with high end properties and the people who buy them."

What is your niche? Every service business and profession has them. Just look at those in your industry, especially the very successful ones. What is their niche? And what niche would you like to develop? Be as specific as you possibly can. I know it seems counter intuitive. But with a smaller, tighter net, you'll catch a lot more fish! Start out small and as you begin to dominate that niche, then you can expand to others. Start by being super laser-focused, committed, and consistent about your marketing efforts into that specific niche.

With my coaching business, at first, I focused on real estate agents. When I got traction with them, I expanded to other people connected with real estate and now I work with all kinds of people who are local businesses and professionals in other industries who have the mindset of an entrepreneur.

One thing we need to understand is that, just because we have niche, we will still do business with people who are not in our niche. Many people are afraid that if they have a niche, that they will lose business. That's just not true, you'll still attract business from all forms, but you specifically attract business that is geared towards your niche. Remember the more our content speaks someone's language, the more they will be attracted towards us. We want our marketing messages to speak the language of the client avatar we are trying to attract.

Your Unique Brand

Okay, you've probably worked with branding and might be thinking, "Hey, I can skip this section." Don't. Your brand isn't just some slick slogan you throw on your flyers. It's not just some spiffy logo or the angle du jour that's supposed to attract hot prospects. It's not just the colors you choose for your website. Your brand can't be some made up version of what you think will sell or who you think people want you to be.

When you think about your brand, forget about fancy business cards or the colors for your website. I want you to first think about how you want people to react to you, to relate to you. Are you the dance instructor who coaches highly talented and motivated students to become pros? Or are you, like dance instructor Nina Koch who emphasizes building life skills in children along with teaching dance skills? Are you the tough negotiator who will get your client as much as possible out of a divorce settlement? Or are you like attorney Carol Delzer whose mission is to create settlements that are fair, cooperative and as amicable as possible? Are you the loan officer who deals with high-end jumbo loans? Or are you like loan officer Debbi Galvan who loves to work with folks who need extra help to get their loans? Your brand has everything to do with who you are, your morals, your values, your personality, your vision, your mission statement, and the benefits you want people to receive from you. What clients are you trying to attract? How will you position yourself in your industry?

And once you determine your brand, that brand should show up in *everything* you do. When I say, "McDonald's," do you get a visual? A feel? A sense of what to expect from that restaurant? Of course, you do. You probably think "casual, family and kids, inexpensive, and convenient," right? Notice that you don't think "high end, fancy, gourmet, expensive." And you know all this even if you've never been to a McDonald's in your entire life! How about Apple? When you think of Apple products, odds are you think "cool, cutting edge, innovative." Compare that with IBM's brand. Totally different, right?

Your brand should be as strong and clear as McDonald's and Apple. It's not about the colors you use or the font on your business cards. Those things are secondary and just support your brand. Your brand is about who you are, the unique value you provide, and the types of clients you want to attract. If you're compassionate, your videos should show compassion. If you're whip-smart, your blogs should be whip-smart. If you're a goof ball, your videos should be humorous.

For example, in the brochures and ads for Nina Koch's dance studio, she features photos of young children dancing. "Other studios might show photos of their more advanced students looking amazing and professional. We have some of those, but that's not really what we're about and who we want to attract. We want kids who will have fun and learn self-confidence and discipline as they build dance skills. So, we highlight the beginners." In Carol Delzer's videos, she'll show divorcing couples sitting and talking with her calmly, even smiling or shaking hands. In those images, both Carol and Nina reinforce what they offer and what they're about. What images would reflect you and your business?

Your brand might change depending on your changing goals or changing circumstances. For example, during the recession several years ago, I realized I had to figure out how to make a living in this new real estate market. I had seen it coming and had started going to trainings and conferences to become an expert at foreclosures. I branded myself that way and became the authority in the foreclosure niche.

When the economy got better, the market went from a foreclosure market to more of a traditional market. One day I lost a listing, so I called the sellers who hadn't chosen me and asked, "Why didn't you choose me?" (This by the way, is a really good practice. Always call and ask if they can give you any constructive criticism about why they didn't choose you. And this is especially important to do if you lose a client!) That seller told me, "We like you. But Krista, the other agent we interviewed said that you were the *foreclosure queen*." That's why they didn't hire me. I had to totally rebrand myself and establish myself as the authority in the market I now wanted. I worked hard at it and within 12 months, I was no longer "the foreclosure queen" but I was the high-end agent who marketed the heck out of her listings using cutting edge technologies. I became "the digital marketing queen."

To be effective, your brand has to sincerely reflect what you're about. It needs to set you apart from the crowd and make you *unforgettable*. Your brand should be in the very DNA of everything about your business, from your business cards, to the way you treat your clients, to the way you market a listing. It's even in the everyday clothes you wear. That means, if you're heading to Starbucks Monday through Friday, 9 to 5, you need to be in the type of business attire that reflects your brand.

Here's the thing: When you start applying the techniques in this book—the technology, community building, and innovation—you'll start getting massive exposure. You don't want an outdated brand and image blasting out to the community. You need to make sure that everything, from your messaging, your niche, your avatar, your photo to your website, reflects the business you are creating. As you adopt and implement the methodologies in this book, you'll get much busier. So, now is the time to get your brand right and start out on the right foot.

To find your unique brand, ask yourself a series of questions: "What is the vision I have for my business? How am I unique? What are my real strengths? How does my market perceive me now and how would I like them to perceive me in the future? What would I like people in my community to say when they tell someone else about me?" "Who is the exact client that I want to attract?"

How do you want people to *feel* about you and your brand? When they see your sign, and when they see your videos, how do you want them to *feel*? For example, when people see my materials,

I want them to feel, "I trust her. I like her. She's real and approachable." Feelings are a huge part of marketing.

People are all over social media nowadays. They want to see anything and everything about you. They look on your social media pages. They see what you're doing. They see what you're interested in. Everything that shows up on your Instagram, Twitter, Snapchat, LinkedIn, and Facebook pages is being watched.

They're interviewing you on social media even when you don't have a clue that they're interviewing you.

Part of your brand is this personal side. People want to get to know you and form a relationship. I love to cook, I love to boat, I love to be on the Delta, and I love entertaining. I show that on my Instagram and my Facebook feeds. I *don't* post anything on those sites that I wouldn't want the world to know or see. I wouldn't post anything that would be detrimental to my brand.

Part of your brand is your personality. I've learned that I don't need to reach the whole world. I only try to reach the people who will connect with me, the people who realize the value of my kind of person. Don't be afraid to be who you are.

As for me, I have tons of energy. I talk fast and think fast. That's just who I am. I can be like a chameleon and slow down when I need to. But, for the most part, my clients love my fast pace. They know I'm going to work quickly in my business and I'm going to get results for them without dragging my feet. Even though I'm fast paced, I still treat my clients like dear, special friends. I take my time with them. I talk *with* my clients, not at them or to them.

I've also worked hard to become very professional at what I do, and I enjoy working with clients who have done the same. I have a lot of education and work well with others who appreciate learning. I also love fun and humor, and I can be crazy at times. I have a degree in Industrial Psychology and a Master's degree in Curriculum and Instruction. I'm a professional so I show up in a professional business suit, but I'm also going to hug my clients, give them a fist bump or a high five, depending on who I'm dealing with. I am a leader, not a follower. I am, and will continue to be, one of those "early adopters" of the latest technology.

As you think about who you really are, also think again about what type of client you want to attract. Who do you want to work with? I want to attract people who respect me both personally and professionally. If someone gets upset that I only have evening appointments one night per week or that I don't handle all aspects of my business but have people on my staff who will contact them, then they aren't the clients I want. If I have a client who is not solution-based and insists on complaining and seeing the bleak side of things, then they aren't the clients I want. I truly am very careful about who I allow into my programs because I know that one Negative Nelly can spread like a deadly virus that wipes out a population.

I've learned the hard way that clients who are the most difficult in the beginning will continue to be that way. They'll demand every ounce of my attention, have little or no regard to my family time, and call at all hours of the night and on weekends. They are showing that they do not respect me, and they are not like me. I respect the business owners and professionals I work with and I also require mutual respect. I have boundaries and I respect other peoples' boundaries. These are the clients I want to attract.

This is important: Be who you want to attract, attract who you want to be. Don't scramble to reach the masses. Reach the people you want to work with. Less is more and more is less, simpler is sweeter.

Your job as a Community Market Leader™ is to develop lasting relationships with people. Your brand does that. It introduces you to people and forms a relationship before you ever meet face to face. When I make educational videos, I show that I have a lot of knowledge and that I'm well-educated. Then I add my bloopers at the end. People get to see my crazy, funny side. They know I'm human. They learn to trust me because I'm giving them value without asking for anything in return, and they like me because I'm a human being, just like them. All of this is part of my brand.

They learn to trust me because I'm giving them value without asking for anything in return, and they like me because I'm a human being, just like them.

Part of my personality is being positive and it's something I value. I show up with a smile and enthusiasm every day. I don't freak out when something unexpected happens but accept it and move on. Am I always feeling like that? No. Am I human? Yes. Do I have bad days? Yes. But I work to shift a negative mindset quickly so I can show up with a positive attitude. People respond positively to positivity. You get what you focus on and I know if I continue to focus on positive outcomes, then I get more of them (this is almost as important if not more than any other aspect of your business).

By the way, if being positive is not in your personality, that's something that will have to change. You don't have to be the bubbly, enthusiastic kind of positive I am. But no one wants to work with a Negative Nellie. Nobody wants to entrust their financial future, their child's education, or their most difficult personal issues to someone who is constantly doom and gloom. A client wants to sit across from a business owner or professional who is confident that he or she can help that client with what they need and want. You might not have a lot of energy like I do. Maybe you're more stoic, analytical, and incredibly smart. That's a strength. Focus on it. Also, people love enthusiasm. The more enthusiastic and passionate you are about what it is that you do and who you serve, the more business and clients you will attract.

Two of my coaching clients who are both loan officers are very different yet they've both been very successful using these strategies. One is easy going, fun loving, and dedicated to her church. Another is more driven and serious, though also fun in her way. What they share is that positive, up-beat, can-do attitude that is so important. And they both say that what has really increased for them through this program is their confidence. They know their potential clients already trust them and see them as an authority.

Your brand is also about your value: a) the value you give and b) the core values you hold. One of my core values is giving back, and every part of who I am expresses that. Like many of the local businesses and professionals in this book, I do a lot of charitable work. I also feel a responsibility to give back in terms of helping train others in my industries, to help them become more professional and more successful. Another of my core values is in my morning affirmations: "I want to positively affect every life that I touch. I want to make sure that my clients feel special, that they know I'm listening to them, and I make time for them." Think about values that are most important to you. Go to http://www.theultimatemarketingplaybook.com/member to see my personal manifesto and a template I created for my students.

As a Community Market Leader™, the value you give is what you do differently. You're an entrepreneur, you treat your business like a business, and you treat your clients with the respect they deserve. You put your *all* into everything you do, you give them your best, and you are a pro. That is the value you give. My team and I have a rule in our office that we always want to be better, and we want to strive for excellence. That's what we do. It shows in our brand, not just as an empty promise, but in everything we do and say.

When I created Homes by Krista, I made sure that I always gave my utmost. I always went above and beyond. Guess what? Word traveled fast. And guess what else? Clients could see that before they met me because in every single thing that I produce, I give value. I have the same attitude in my coaching business. I'm determined to help my students succeed and am constantly looking for new ways bring out their best. I'm dedicated to being authentic with them, and sometimes that means that I have to be willing to get in their face or give them a kick in the butt.

What value do you bring to the table? What qualities represent you, your business, your business model, and what you produce for your clients? What benefits do you give your clients that is different from your competitors?

As you become a Community Market Leader™ and start to dominate your market, part of your brand will be just that: You're a community leader who dominates his or her market. You're going to be seen and known everywhere. So, part of your brand will be, "Wow, I see that person everywhere." Make sure that your brand is really clear and really *you* before it starts showing up as you everywhere.

When you're thinking about your brand, start with how you want your community to react to you, how you want them to receive you, how you want them to relate to you, and how you want to build trust with them. Really think about your strengths, personality, and the value you bring. Once you are clear about all those things, only then is it time to look into logos, business cards, and the colors and photos on your website. Don't make the mistake of trying to create these pieces first before really knowing your brand.

If you are new in your business, you still need to develop your brand. It's not set in stone and it probably will change. Even so, you want to start standing out from the pack. What I don't recommend is that you try to promote yourself as having more experience or knowledge than you actually have. Being dishonest will come back to bite you. People come to you as a professional because they need help with something important. Be clear about your skills and knowledge.

Instead of presenting yourself as highly experienced and knowledgeable, you can say something like this: "I am a relatively new landscape architect. But let me tell you what makes me different than any other landscape architect: I am innovative and I'm doing things differently than the people who have been in the business for fifteen to twenty years. I'm up to speed with how climate changes might affect your landscape and how to design for that. I've been trained in new and more efficient watering systems. And because I'm just building my reputation, I will be 100% dedicated to making sure you are thrilled with what I put together for you."

If you were approached in that way, wouldn't you respect it and be attracted by it? Dale Carnegie wrote a classic book called *How to Win Friends and Influence People*. In it, he points out that people like to do business with people that they like. And prospective clients are going to like you if they can see that you're ethical, dedicated, determined, and that you sincerely have their best interests at heart.

> *people like to do business with people that they like. And prospective clients are going to like you if they can see that you're ethical, dedicated, determined, and that you sincerely have their best interests at heart.*

People do not always choose the first service provider they interview, whether it's an attorney, a therapist, or an architect. If you get a foot in the door, don't waste it. Be likable, be honest, and have integrity. Give them as much value and knowledge in that first appointment as possible. Don't be stingy with your knowledge. This is all part of your new brand.

Stay Ahead of the Trends

What I'm going to say next may sound contradictory to the last sections. Bear with me.

Creating your niche is critical to your success. But don't be swimming upstream in the market. Get *ahead* of the market by knowing what's coming down the pike. What do I mean by that? Economic markets, demographics, and issues change. And you've got to change with them.

For example, say you're an architect who specializes in very high-end vacation homes design. You follow economic trends nationally and locally and you see tough times, maybe a recession coming down the pike. When that happens, you know that vacation homes won't be such a hot commodity. Now what? This is where you need to be flexible. What is another niche you could tap? Maybe it's renovations rather than new construction. Maybe it's designing in-law's cottages on high-end properties for all those kids and grandparents who are moving back in. Think out of the box.

Even in the beginning of my career, I always researched market trends. I tried to anticipate, based upon data and analytics, how the real estate market would be affected in the future. In the years 2005-2007, we had a fantastic seller's market. Suddenly, I realized that home prices were increasing too fast. Common sense told me that something was going to happen.

I started researching loans and trends in the market. I figured out people would soon start losing their homes. I knew we were going to have a problem. I started contacting banks, traveling the country, and going to bankers' association conferences. By the time the real estate market completely crashed in 2008, by being proactive and thinking ahead, I landed over thirteen banks and asset management companies, and helped them sell their foreclosures and short sales.

I continued to keep my finger on the pulse of the market. By 2014, values were getting closer to where values had been previously. I could see the foreclosures lessening and asset management companies selling off their portfolios to larger banks. It seemed likely that we'd have a more traditional market within six to twelve months. So, it was time for me to reposition myself from a foreclosure and short sale specialist, to an area specialist in high end properties. This was prompted by the "foreclosure queen" incident.

None of this happened by accident. I paid attention and I used common sense to anticipate what was going to happen. Then I positioned myself to respond to what was happening before most agents in the market even realized it was changing. The difference was anticipation and preparation.

Your business or profession may not be quite as volatile as real estate can be. But whatever your business or profession, it will undoubtedly change over the course of your career (especially in the case of a pandemic). Think about it. How many Blockbuster video stores do you see these days? At its peak in 2004, Blockbuster had more than 4500 video stores in the U.S. and nearly 9,100 worldwide. It filed for bankruptcy in 2010 and closed its last company-owned 300 stores in 2013. As of 2019, there is just one franchise Blockbuster still open. What the heck happened?

Technology happened.

First came Netflix with its mail-order video service. Next came video on demand and today it's all about streaming videos. Blockbuster did not anticipate and prepare for these changes. It stubbornly kept with the same model it had always used rather than adopting the new technologies. Netflix had the potential to become obsolete as well. The company was a little slow on the trigger when streaming started eating into their market share. But the company regrouped and joined the bandwagon of streaming then even started creating content of its own to keep up with other streaming services. Netflix anticipated and prepared. Blockbuster did not.

Stay flexible. Without giving up your core values or the overall vision for your business, stay responsive to market conditions. Educate yourself about the market: What's happening? What's going on in the community, locally? What's happening nationally? What are the new trends in your business or profession? How does that affect what's happening now and what could possibly happen later?

And how can your business remain responsive to all of that?

Innovation

We've talked about this, but I'm going to say it again because it's critical: Once you have the vision of what kind of business you're creating and have a clear idea of your brand, you need to start incorporating innovation in all you do. If you don't, no matter how competent you are, you'll get left behind.

When I first started, one agent in our community completely ruled the market. It was unimaginable that anyone would ever be able to hold as much market share as this powerhouse agent. Today, that powerhouse is still in the ranking, but I've surpassed that person by far. Even within my first year of being in business, I was neck in neck with this fierce competitor. The same thing happened in my coaching and training business. In my first year, I surpassed a guy who had been in the coaching business in my area for several years. Why? Because I chose to be different and innovative. Don't be like everyone else who uses the same old approach that was used two, five, ten, fifteen, or twenty years ago. Do things differently, be a leader, set the new norm, and stand out from the crowd. The very cool thing is that as soon as your competitors take notice of just how different you've become and how you've set the "new norm," you'll already be holding market share and your business will have a momentum that is unstoppable.

My goal is to make sure that you understand how to be innovative and stay at the top of your marketplace. It's like cell phones. When they first came out forty years ago, they weighed 2½ pounds, died after 20 minutes of use, and cost about $3,000. Twenty years later, cell phones could be used as pagers, fax machines, and PDAs (personal digital assistants) to store phone numbers and keep track of your calendar. Today, you can use a cell phone to pay for Starbucks, navigate your way across town, find out the latest baseball scores, talk to someone on video and book a trip across the world. (In 2013, the UN reported there were more people on earth with mobile phones (six billion for world population of seven billion) than there are with access to clean toilets (only 4.5 billion).)

If the cell phone industry can change that much, don't you think your industry should evolve as well? Look at what's happened to travel agents. They are practically extinct now because technology has taken over. The great service and knowledge these people had has been traded for convenience and speed. It's up to us as service professionals to make sure that our unique value doesn't get replaced by some clever app someone invents!

Those of us who choose to be different, innovative, and beyond wonderful will not only survive but thrive. Yes, even during a pandemic or bad economy. You can't afford to be "just good." You have to be excellent, superb, and beyond great. You need to outshine everyone with your creativity, innovation, drive and customer service driven work ethic!

Steve Jobs said, "Innovation distinguishes between a leader and a follower." The definition of innovation from BusinessDictionary.com is, *"The process of translating an idea or invention into a good or service, that creates value, or for which consumers will pay. To be called an **innovation**, an idea must be replicable at an economical cost and must satisfy a specific need."*

Basically, innovation is to find out some new idea, device, or method. It's the application of better solutions that meet new requirements and articulated needs, or existing market needs.

Technovation

A big part of being innovative is adopting technologies that can make your business more efficient. It's about understanding how people today are finding mortgages, yoga studios, or financial planner and using that information—and technology— to design where and how you market your services. It's about using every new app available to you, implementing them in your business, and updating them on a regular basis.

Typically, you can find reports and statistics about how people shop for different services online: how they do their searches, what devices they use for their searches, what people find valuable when searching for your service, and what information they find valuable on websites. Often, your business or professional organizations will have such data.

Innovation isn't just about technology. Sometimes you can come up with an idea that is better than the technology available to you. For example, a few years back, I ran into a certain real estate software that you upload on an iPad. Potential buyers enter the house and click on the iPad as they walk into each room and it tells them about the features. It is a good app, but time consuming and not very user-friendly. I tried it for a while then quit using it.

But it gave me an idea. I found someone to make very specific videos, and we hone in on the home's upgrades. I have that video available in the home, and also use it on the home's website and on social media so many more people are exposed to it. I use a professional videographer, so the quality is excellent. This video tour gets blasted out for the whole internet world to see.

Get Cozy with Failure, Not your Comfort Zone

I always encourage people to fail! What I mean by that is that you have to be willing to try new things and, if they don't work, learn from the experience and move on. Too many people are fearful of failure, so they stay within their comfort zone and avoid being innovative. The comfort zone is *not* your friend! Not every technology you use or idea you have will be successful. There isn't a thing I haven't tried. I've tried it all and I've failed plenty of times before I succeeded. I often figured out what *could* work by doing something that *didn't*. If you aren't failing with some of your ideas, you probably aren't stretching far enough out of the box.

Every very successful person I've ever known has failed a number of times. Take dance studio owner Nina Koch. Years ago, she had been in a marketing group where the guru of that group swore by door hangers. So, Nina spent a ton of money producing these fantastic door hangers and getting them distributed. "We put out thousands of them and got absolutely zero response. I tried it again. Nothing. After the third time with no response, I talked to the guy who had suggested it. He said, 'Oh, door hangers don't work in California where you are.' But I was actually stubborn enough to try it one more time! From this experience, I've learned to pay attention to my results. Just because something works great for someone else, doesn't mean it's going to work for me."

Attorney Carol Delzer talks about trying TV spots several years ago. "I got a script writer and brought some amateur actors. The TV station brought their professional camera crew. The spots were really well done, and I was very proud of them. But you know what? After running them for several months, I don't think we got even one client from them." The good news is that Carol realized she had some great footage she could use elsewhere. "Now I edit it and use it on my website, in Facebook posts and ads, all kinds of ways."

I started a homeowner's support program after the real estate market tanked. I thought I could help people in distress and that it would help me financially make it through the real estate downturn. I put a lot of time and money into creating the program, but it didn't pan out in the way I'd hoped. However, I did help some people. I didn't get a lot of business from that strategy, but I had the satisfaction of helping people work through their real estate challenges. Through the program, I was able to help people save their homes and find alternatives to short sale or foreclosure. But once I took into account all of my costs, personnel and time, I really didn't make any money on it.

Since the program didn't pay off as I wanted, I made a video. I don't get contacted by many people who are having these real estate difficulties nowadays. But that video is still online and will be seen forever! That one strategy didn't work out as I'd planned, but others did. **Do not give up!** Keep trying and manipulating what you are doing.

As Glenn Hoffman says of his insurance business, "I made every mistake in the book, from hiring and how to train, to how to control the finances. But it's just a matter of learn from the mistake. Stand up, brush your knees off, and try again. And hopefully not repeat that same mistake."

It's okay to fail. It's okay to try something that doesn't end up working. I've failed five times to succeed once. But if you're focused on innovation, that one success will totally outweigh all the failures.

Take the Next Step

1. *Go to the example branding and avatar worksheets at http://www.theultimatemarketingplaybook.com/member. Use these to start creating your brand and niche.*

2. *Grab a piece of paper and write "The Business I'd Love to Have" at the top. Without censoring yourself or worrying about how you'll get there, write down how your perfect business would look.*

CHAPTER FIVE

MARKETING: IT'S MORE THAN LEADS

The next few chapters are all about marketing in the 21st century. I absolutely love marketing! Whether you do or not, it's the oxygen that will keep your business thriving. Without it, you're DOA—dead on arrival!

First of all, before you even take the first step in marketing, you need to have done the work we talked about in Chapter Four. You need to have your brand defined and know who your target market is. Without these two things in place, you'll be flying all over creation, spending time and money on approaches that have nothing to do with the people you're trying to attract. With your branding, niche and target market defined, you're going to save money, and you're going to reach more people, and you're actually going to get more clients during your conversion phase. You'll know exactly what content to produce and your marketing message will speak directly to your target market.

Also, as you read the next chapters about marketing and the sales cycle, I want you to come up with a rough plan. Your plan will get clearer as you learn and implement the steps. At this stage, start by figuring out how much time you'll devote to marketing and what your rough budget for this is. Most people end up realizing that marketing takes way more time, energy and money than they thought, especially at the beginning. Given that this piece will make or break your business, think about how you can make marketing a priority. Remember, input equals output. What you're willing to give/spend determines what you'll get out of it. So how much time are you willing to put into it? How much money are you willing to invest? What strategy and what system are you going to employ? As you read the next chapters, don't just sit back and be passive. Use the information I'm giving you to develop your plan.

This first marketing chapter is all about leads. Before we talk about leads, it's important to understand the *complete* sales cycle. It's a huge concept that most professionals and small businesses overlook which causes 95% of them to fail or, if they survive, they remain stagnant. With these 6 phases of a complete sales cycle, your potential clients or customers end up not only working with you but staying with you as a client forever. The six phases are as follows: Phase one is **marketing, followed by lead generation,** then comes **lead nurture, then conversion, then fulfillment** and **delivery**. And finally, but importantly, the last stage is **refer, retain**, and **resell** (and I've recently added rituals and routines which simply means the things you do to remain consistent). To make sure you achieve the success you want in whatever industry, make sure you're focused on every single aspect of the sales cycle.

Think of it like a romance. I don't think most of us are going to jump in bed with someone after the first get-to-know-you coffee date. You might like the guy or gal, but you probably want a little more information and familiarity and trust before you take that leap, right? The first stages of the sales cycle are kinda like dating. You're not forcing the issue for an immediate "sale." You're letting them get to know you and trust you.

When I talk about the complete sales cycle, I always recite the 9 C's: You've got to **commit** to **consistently,** producing **content** the **correct way** so you'll make a **connection** with people, then you're more likely to **convert** them into **clients** and if you **continue** with this **cycle**, you have the **complete** sales system.

*When I talk about the complete sales cycle, I always recite the 9 C's: You've got to **commit** to **consistently,** producing **content** the **correct way** so you'll make a **connection** with people, then you're more likely to **convert** them into **clients** and if you **continue** with this **cycle**, you have the **complete** sales system.*

Tattoo that on your forehead (backwards so you can read it in the mirror!).

Marketing and Lead Generation: The Art of Attraction

I'm known as the queen of digital marketing in my area and in my business. That's probably why I know that generating leads is *so* easy! I use the power of the internet. If someone ever tells you that getting good leads is hard, trust me, they're going about it in the wrong way. I'd like you to really understand that getting leads is simple, simple, simple!

What is lead generation? Lead generation is defined as "methods and activities for offering something of value in exchange for contact information to add to your database." In other words, I'm going to give you something you want (a lead "magnet") so that you'll give me your name and phone number, or just your email address or just your name (whatever contact information you want). Many professionals and businesses pay for leads and lead sources, but they're not giving back anything of value to that lead. In engagement marketing, the emphasis is on giving value, serving, not selling. Of course, when you serve really well, ultimately you sell. Keep the service mindset in the forefront and selling will follow. To generate leads, the most important factor is the platform or platforms you utilize.

When you're utilizing your platform, are you going to be online? I hope so! Carol Delzer, the divorce mediation attorney, tells a story about waking up to online marketing and the internet. About 15 years ago, her daughter Jessica worked in Carol's office as a summer intern. One day, Jessica asked her mom, "What's this "Yellow Pages" fee you're paying?" Carol explained that it was for her ads in the Yellow Pages." Jessica was floored. "Mom! No one uses the Yellow Pages anymore!" She's right. Whether they're looking for an attorney, a plumber, a therapist or a yoga studio, everybody gets on the internet these days. The Yellow Pages may have worked 25 years ago, but it's not where you want to be spending your money now! (The good news is that Carol's daughter spent the summer getting her website updated, setting up a blog, and basically bringing her mom into the 21st century!)

When you're online, you can be utilizing landing pages, doing email campaigns, creating a great website, getting involved in social media and search engine optimization (SEO). For social media, you might use Facebook or YouTube or Instagram or LinkedIn, whichever is the right platform for your target audience. If you're a b2b (business selling to another business) business or profession, LinkedIn is your best bet. People under 30 tend to gravitate to Instagram, so if you're a restaurant or sell clothing aiming towards millennials, that would be your platform. Older people will be on Facebook. The platforms change over time so be sure and research the best for you. (For more information on platforms, go to http://www.theultimatemarketingplaybook.com/member.)

Keep in mind, people are online (and that includes grandmas and grandpas!) They do research online. They buy stuff online. They seek information online. They look for testimonials online. They look at their grandkids' latest photos online. Unless your target market lives in some super-remote place with no internet connection, your target audience is online, at least to some extent.

You'll also want to utilize more traditional platforms like the magazine or newspaper ads and articles, giving personal presentations, networking at community organizations, hosting holiday parties and open houses, or supporting community non-profits, schools, and good causes. All of these are lead-generating sources. However, if you're utilizing some of those old school strategies that people did ten years ago, ask yourself two questions: 1. Are the results you're getting from each of these activities worth the energy/time/money you're putting into it? 2. Are you doing that old school activity in a way that is fresh, innovative, and engaging?

The personal connection you get with some of these old school strategies is great. And honestly, the best overall marketing plans include both in-person and digital strategies. However, if your business is national, that's not always possible. Just keep in mind that you can also get a personal feel using video as well. Being online doesn't mean being impersonal.

Once you've picked your online platform, next you want to figure out some great lead magnets for your digital strategy. Magnets can be things like

eBooks, videos with valuable content, Facebook Lives, white papers, landing pages with digital or valuation calculators (for example, "How much home can you afford?" or "How much do you need to retire?"), Facebook groups—basically anything that people would find attractive enough to exchange their contact information so they can get it. You can offer these things at in-person events as well.

By the way, can you already feel how different this is than the old school approach? You're not showing up at someone's door, trying to convince them to want what you offer. You're not chasing ambulances or stalking small business owners to do their tax returns, design their offices, or handle their HR. People are *coming to you* because they *want* what you've got. When you show up at networking or community events, you won't have to talk people into taking your eCard, business card or flyer. They'll demand it from you!

Tracie Schmidt, a loan officer in my program, will tell you that she used to chase after agents, and now agents are chasing after her. They want to work with her because they're seeing her out there. When I go to conferences, people seek me out to ask about my coaching and training programs. They're thinking, "Wow. I see Krista everywhere. I want to be part of that."

Attorney Carol Delzer distributes her book *Divorce Made Easy* for free to therapists in her area. People going to those therapists see the book in the waiting room and glance through it. If they decide to divorce, they instantly think of Carol. She was encouraged by her daughter to start blogging, making sure that the blogs rank high on SEO. Now Carol loves blogging, saying that it helps her think more globally and rekindles her passion for what she does. When new clients call, they often refer to one of her blogs.

Yoga coach Raquel Otis offers two full weeks of yoga training with her via live video for free on www.RaquelOtis.com/spark.

After people have taken their two weeks, she transitions them into her paid yoga coaching programs.

In another example, writer Heather Estay had written her first screenplay and posted it with an online service but she had no idea what to do next. She noticed a free online webinar from an online training company called ScreenwritingU. The webinar was titled "How Screenwriters Over Fifty Can Make It in the Movie Business" and she was intrigued and signed up (Yes, she admits to being well over fifty!). The webinar was incredibly well done, and she took a bunch of notes. In fact, she got so much good information from it, that when a producer called the next week, she knew exactly what to say to land the deal and sell her script! She immediately signed up for several ScreenwritingU classes. That's the power of giving real value, folks!

Obviously, there are a bunch of different ways to ensure that you get more leads. Having a really good offer, having a great hook, telling a great story, and then reeling them in via your funnel. You want to make sure that you're identifying exactly who your specific client is (your avatar, Chapter Four), where they hang out, what they do, and what they like, identifying their pain and pleasure and marketing to that. Once you know that and you create the right free content or informational videos, getting your leads is as easy as giving candy to a baby, and I absolutely mean that.

Consistency: Rinse and Repeat

Whether you're generating leads online or in more old school ways, two major keys are *consistency* and *intention*. You can't just put out one informational video or blog and expect leads/people to come pouring in. You can't just do one webinar and expect to fill your school or your client roster. You have to be consistent so that people see you again and again.

It's also important that you focus on a) lead generation vehicles that get results, and b) lead generation vehicles that work for *you* and that fit who you are.

Tiffany Rose, a loan officer with Guild Mortgage, has learned this lesson with the events she attends in person. "There is this one amazing wine and cheese networking opportunity I attended a couple of times. But I realized that I don't belong there. It was too much business promotion and not enough connection for me. So, I found some others that fit me better. You have to find your own jam." At these mixers, Tiffany focuses on serving people and really getting to know them. "To do that, you can't just attend the mixer once or twice. You need to show up consistently and participate. Be confident and serve people. If you walk in and target someone because you want business out of them, that is absolutely the wrong approach. Energetically you're going to come through differently than you would if you were just wanting to get to know people and make friends."

Tiffany also talks about really getting to know people at these events, so you know if they're the right fit for you and someone you want to work with. "I want to work with good people. And you can only find out if they're good people, if you go to the event consistently, whether it's an annual chili cook-off or the weekly real estate marketing meeting. You can't expect people to fall in love with you if you only show up every once in a while." Because of her consistency and her intention to serve, Tiffany gets a "flood of leads" from the events she attends.

"It doesn't have to be painful," Tiffany says. "I just had to figure out what makes sense for me and my life and my family. If it's too painful, you're probably not using the right strategies."

Tracie Schmidt has also seen the power of consistency. "I'd been doing videos for years, but I only did them only every once in a while. After I began Krista's course, I started producing them on a regular basis and distributed them correctly and consistently. Krista showed me how to properly get my content out there so people actually saw my content. The leads I got from doing that was like night and day compared to the results I'd had in the years before."

In the 9 C's I talked about earlier, consistency is one of the most important keys. You're not going to get far by being sporadic in your efforts, just marketing and engaging when you feel like it. You need to be consistent, day after day, week after week. That's when, like Tracie, you'll see the results you're looking for.

Consistency is all about developing small habits and planning. Habits are things you do without even consciously deciding to do it, like brushing your teeth before you go to bed. Most of us would feel weird if we *didn't* brush our teeth, right? But we didn't start out that way. For most of us as kids, our parents first had to show us how to do it then they had to nag us to do it until finally it became a habit. I've heard that it takes 21 days to form a habit. So, for the first 21 days of doing the things I'm asking you to do, including these videos, you'll have to remind yourself. You'll have to keep those tasks on your calendar and put it on your daily To Do list. You'll have to prioritize them over other activities you might be used to doing. You'll have to remind yourself of why you're doing them. Then you'll just have to do them, whether you feel like it or not! That's where your commitment comes in. After a while, especially when you start seeing results, you'll be eager to create videos and content and get them distributed correctly!

It may seem like a huge thing at first. One thing I do when I have a project that feels big is to break it down into mini commitments. For instance, when I have a big speech or presentation coming up, I don't sit down one day and try to knock the whole thing out. That's just too overwhelming. Instead, I set myself up to work on it for 25 minutes increments a few times a day, every single day for two weeks. I put that "appointment" on my calendar and honor it as if I'm meeting with a client. I chip away at the speech over that two weeks and guess what? By the end, I've got a really good draft that just needs polishing. And because I made it into a routine, my subconscious was already working on that speech even when I wasn't consciously working on it and is ready to go when I sit down to actually do it.

You can talk yourself into doing just about anything a few times a day for 20-25 minutes, right? People who hate exercise often use the mini-commitment idea to get themselves started. They'll tell themselves, "Okay, I'm just going to work out for 15 minutes." But by the time they've exercised for a few minutes, they start feeling good and are really into it. They keep going. If they do this day after day, they start to find that they don't have so much resistance to exercising at all. They've created a habit. They've become consistent and, just like everything we do, that consistency is what pays off. If they did a spurt of exercise for a few days then slacked off for the rest of the month, do you think they'd see any results? No. And it's the same with your marketing.

It's About Quality

Let me say this again: The quality of your marketing whether online or more traditional, reflects both on the quality of your business and you personally. Quality doesn't necessarily have to do with flashy graphics or a gorgeous website (though, if you have the capacity to do that, it's helpful!) It has to do with: a) making sure your content is awesome

> *The quality of your marketing whether online or more traditional, reflects both on the quality of your business and you personally.*

and directly connects with your target market, and b) making sure your content can be found.

For example, let's talk about creating the website. For those of you who aren't familiar with SEO (search engine optimization), it's basically one of the ways people find you online. When you Google something like "homemade toothpaste," the search engines hunt for words that most closely match what you want to find. SEO figures out what words people use most often to find whatever you have. So, in our example, statistics might show that words like "natural," "teeth," "toothpaste," and "homemade" are the words people most often put in that search box. With SEO, you take that information and make sure that your descriptions and titles use the most popular words so your business will pop up on the first page of someone's search. Using the correct words to describe your videos, websites, blogs, or online ads will ensure you have higher ranking in the search engines and that your target market will find you. This applies to Facebook, social media target market specific ads, your website, and anything you put online. (There is a lot of technology and information behind SEO and it could take up an entire chapter in itself. One quick helpful hint is to make sure you add a title to all of your pictures.)

Basically, a pixel is a tracking cookie that follows potential clients online so when they click on your ads, posts, websites or links, they start to automatically get your future videos, posts and updates. Don't freak out! This is so simple that anyone can do it. You'll just need a little training. Using pixels on a platform like Facebook, you can create a "Target Audience" and "Look Alike Audiences." There is massive opportunity here and by paying for ads to promote you, your product or service, that is how we see business owners and professionals make massive impact, very quickly. The problem is most people don't know how to do it or the strategy behind it, and that is why they fail so often. You can rely on organic reach, but it will take you long and rarely do posts or content go viral without paying for exposure. I specialize in teaching businesses how to do this. (To learn more about how we can help you or your business go to www.KristaMashore.com/BizBump.)

If you want to do quality marketing, most likely you'll have to spend more than the average person in your business or profession spends. But it doesn't have to break the bank. When implementing some of these ideas or ideas you come up with on your own, stop and really think about how you can get the job done cost effectively before you plunge in. As you start to make more money, which you will, start to add and expand. Learn, Implement, Master, Repeat. Always focus on getting better and better and improving/ innovating. Repeat what you're learning because as things evolve, we need to continue to improve.

> *Learn, Implement, Master, Repeat. Always focus on getting better and better and improving/innovating.*

When I go to conferences now, I often run into someone who has read my books or listened to my podcasts. They'll come up and tell me how much they got out of it and how it changed their lives in some way. When I was focused on real estate, I'd walk into a house and the homeowner would pull out some great marketing piece I did years before. "I kept this because it was so different and nice. I'd never seen one like this, so I thought to myself, 'When I sell, I'm going to call her.'"

Slaying Cyberspace

Obviously, I do a lot to tap into the power of social media and the internet. If you are just starting in this type of marketing, don't become overwhelmed by it. Take it piece by piece. Your goal is to improve. Start with an ad or a webinar or a blog and track its results (which may not be instant). Then, implement a new technology that will enhance your exposure, maybe doing a video blog the next time. The key is consistency. Once you master and implement an innovation or technology, keep doing it and add more. Don't stop with the first attempt but keep adding to it. Keep in mind that technologies are changing constantly so you'll need to keep track if something new and improved is out there that can better serve your clients and in turn better serve you.

> *The key is consistency. Once you master and implement an innovation or technology, keep doing it and add more.*

Some of what I do today seems expensive, like spending $200 on a specific ad campaign on Facebook. But if that ad generates 75,000 to 125,000-views, or 234 to 655 hours of watch time in a two week period, to me it's totally worth it. However, I didn't start there. I added the extra investment into marketing my business as it grew.

For each video that I produce—whether for my real estate business or my training and coaching business—I am creating a target audience, re-targeting audience or lookalike audience for my campaigns. I'm showing up wherever they are and redirecting them to what I want my audience to see. You're creating an *audience*, not targeting one person. Anyone who's ever looked at your videos, or anyone who's ever researched you, they all become a part of your target audience. You start showing up on their feed, on their computer—anywhere they go, you're there. Then automatically, you redirect them to see that next thing you want them to see.

Cultivate Your Community Creatively

I, along with everyone we interviewed for this book, am very involved in community and community service. It turns out we're all givers and, though this is a huge advantage to us in business, we would be givers whether it helped our businesses or not.

Whatever you do, do it differently and offer as much value as possible. If you sponsor a community event, don't show up with tacky pens and flyers promoting how great you are. Show up with calendars of upcoming fun events, city sports team schedules (in my area Raiders, 49'ers, A's, Giants), or a contact list of places to volunteer in the community. If you organize a food drive, how about doing it in the summer rather than the holidays when everyone else does theirs? Maybe you can collect the extra vegetables and fruit people have in their own gardens rather than asking for cans. Or, you can set up a competition between schools, giving a prize to whichever school collects the most food.

One of my students Alisha Collins does an "Adopt a Pet" series where she partners with a local humane society. She picks a dog a week to sponsor and runs an ad to find a home for it. She's gotten tons of exposure due to this. She didn't do it to get exposure, she did it to give back to the community and she LOVES DOGS. Another student, Kim Renshaw did an "Adopt a Road" where the adopter is responsible for picking up trash on the roadside. She cleans up specific roads in her community which have signs that say, "Road adopted by Kim Renshaw Family." Now she has dozens of people helping her pick up trash on those roads—and of course she's picked up clients as well.

One super popular theme day that I created for my community was, "Vision Board Making Day." I created a video showing what a vision board is and why it's so important. Then, I invited the entire community to come to my office and make their vision boards with me. Lots of people showed up and everyone just loved it. Even better, I was able to help participants see a roadmap of their goals and add value to them.

Financial planner Carol Van Bruggen gives back by serving on several Boards in her community, from the Music Circus in Sacramento to Capital Public Radio. "Not only do I get to know other businesses and professionals in the community and form relationships. I've also gotten great experience in planning and dealing with conflicts and difficult situations the organization might be facing." Carol also enjoys participating in service groups like Rotary. "I don't go into these groups expecting direct referrals. But being part of these service organizations has been very satisfying and has built my reputation in the community." Carol even ended up starting her own non-profit, Africa Hope Fund, that works with organizations in Zambia to protect wildlife and educate local Zambian children.

Insurance broker Glenn Hoffman is also a big giver. "I give a lot to charity from the agency. We also own a restaurant, so we give gift cards to help organizations raise funds in raffles or auctions. Virtually anyone who asks with a valid charity, I will make a donation. I'm also the president of the Lions Club and we give literally a six-figure donation back to our local community in the surrounding areas every year." Does Glenn do this just to market his business? No. His intention is to give back to the community that has given him so much.

For me personally, I've been fortunate enough to make a very good living so I can give back. I've created several events that give the proceeds to a child with cancer or donate money to a family who lost a child. For example, here is the post I used for the "Amazing Race" event I created:

I am at the point in my life where I want to be more *intentional* about giving back. Everything in my studies and research emphasizes giving as much as I can to clients and people around me—and not letting my fear

> *when an idea hits you, grasp it, go for it, and be intentional about implementing your idea.*

of people stand in the way of helping and adding value. In *Think and Grow Rich*, Napoleon Hill wrote that, when an idea hits you, grasp it, go for it, and be intentional about implementing your idea. In one part, he noted that if kids in schools were required to read his book, it would reduce the time it took them to learn any subject by half. He thought it should be mandatory to read the book prior to graduating high school.

Immediately, a green light went off in my head. I was getting ready for work and listening to the audio book of *Think and Grow Rich*. I immediately stopped what I was doing, went to the computer, and typed out my idea. It was the seed idea of the program I created called *Teens Lifting Lives*. Here's what I wrote on a Facebook post (I also created a video):

$1,000 for TWENTY Young Minds Ages of 15 to 19 who live in Brentwood, Oakley, Antioch, or Discovery Bay who will read the book (or Audio Book) Think & Grow Rich from Napoleon Hill & be willing to commit to the Following for the next 8 weeks: If you are reading this please share. 🙂

Here are the details and requirements:

p.s. this is a drug and alcohol-free program. I know that students from time to time may dabble in this; however, the commitment is that each student must take an oath and abide by it that they will keep 100% free of drugs and alcohol during this 8-week program and not be afraid to take a stand and voice their stance of being "Drug and Alcohol FREE" to those around them, even when being tempted or having peer pressure.

1. *Will Read One Chapter each week, No More No Less and apply the skills and methodologies that he suggests.*
2. *Have a willingness to have an Open Mind and Desire to want to better yourself and add Value to others.*
3. *Will spend 25% of the $1,000 by Paying it Forward to ANY cause that will make a difference in the life of someone else. (You'll need to think about this and let me know in your application)*
4. *Promise to be a person in the community, whether it be at school or home, that has a standard of excellence in how they treat others (no bullies here, if you are a bully or gossiper, you'll have to stop for the 8 weeks, this is imperative).*
5. *If Chosen: Join the Facebook Group w/ the other 19 participants and give your feedback, support, and commitment to the other members in the Face Book Group for the 8 weeks.*
6. *Be willing to Earn the $1,000 by doing the homework that will be required each week (no more than two hours). This is*

dedicated to time of learning the book and applying the principles of Personal Growth and Development for oneself and the community (your efforts will be evaluated, if the effort is not put in, we will be giving your $1,000 to the charity of your choice).

7. *Meet every Tuesday via zoom video from 6:00-7:00 a.m. to review the book and share experiences*
8. *Have one full day of no social media or phone each week.*
9. *No social media, internet, or phone for 1 hour each day.*
10. *Meet for four hours to do goal setting w/ the group prior to the session starting.*
11. *Join in a Graduation Ceremony at the end where you will tell the members in the group and their families how reading the book has changed you and make a Vision Board*

Hint Hint, Reading Chapter 2 will help you in getting chosen. Definiteness of Purpose and having the Desire to Possess it will help you get chosen.*

*** Please apply by sending your application to Krista@KristaHomes.com*** Applications are due Monday February 13th and the program will start on Wednesday February 15th. You will be notified if you made it on Monday February 13th.***

There may be 2-3 times the group will meet for an hour together to master mind and share.

Please only apply if you are serious and dedicated to 8 weeks of improving yourself and others that surround you. Please apply only if you will commit to making a difference in yourself and others. This is NOT about making the money, but about making a difference.

I am dedicated to running this Program as often as I can, so if you do not make it in the first round, you'll get another opportunity. My hope is that by my adding value to you, you will in turn add value to those around you!!

Application Requirements:

1. *Desire: Clearly define your desire. Exactly WHY do you want to be in the program? How will it help you and others? Visualize this and see yourself here.*

2. *Explain exactly what you will give in return for being in the program and who/what you will give the 25% of your money to. ($250 of the $1,000)*
3. *Explain how you Plan on making the time to read/listen to one chapter a week and apply the principles without it affecting your school.*
4. *Pledge to be 100% committed to this and your cause in writing.*
5. *One and only one letter of recommendation as to why you would be great for this. Remember, you don't have to be a model citizen. If you are struggling with something and feel this class will help you, please apply. This is not just for the perfect students in the world, lol. It's for everyone (hey, when I was young, I was actually in juvenile hall, so we all can change!).*

***Only the first 50 Applications will be looked at. Please keep your application down to one page. (Please type it, it will make it easier on me. lol)

Good Luck Kids! Let's make a difference together!!!

Please email your applications to:

Krista@KristaHomes.com

Sincerely,

Krista

I'm committed to taking on students for as long as I can and, so far, I've been able to continue this since I started. This program has been a lot of work but it's so fulfilling. I get a kick out of it, and the impact the program is making on the kids is amazing. Not for one second did I say or think, "I'm going to do this to promote my businesses." It was purely to give and serve. However, you can't imagine all the buzz I've gotten from it.

My point is that I created this program to help, to serve, to give back. In turn, it's helping me both personally and professionally. I am grateful to these kids for allowing me to experience such joy and fulfillment. To see how these young people grow and change over the eight weeks is even more rewarding.

So, you can see there are lots and lots of ways to generate leads. It's easy peasy and can be fun and truly satisfying. The harder part is phase number two: lead nurturing. Read on.

CHAPTER SIX

LEAD NURTURE TO CONVERSION

So, you've got tons of leads coming in. Now what? Depending on what type of company you work for or business you have, in most cases, people are not just calling up or walking right into your office right away and saying, "Hey, I want to work with you right now." People, especially these days, do their research. So, once you actually get that lead, you want to nurture it by helping them to feel comfortable with you, to know you, to like you, to trust you, to want to work with you, and to being top-of-mind awareness for them. Understand that when somebody reaches out to you or engages in some form by looking you up on social media or going to your website or even requesting one of your lead magnets, they're not usually ready to work with you right away. That's why the lead nurturing process is so imperative.

To really have a great lead nurturing process, it's very important that you have a very good CRM (customer relations manager) and that you're constantly making contact with them. What forms of contact should you be making? Emailing, phone calling, text messaging, video text messaging, video emailing, and in-person as much as possible. And it's communicating, not just to say, "Hi. Remember me?" It's to offer valuable information that you've already developed in your funnel. Or it can be answering their specific questions or offering to serve in some way. Yes, it can be a lot of work (though much of it can be pre-planned and automated). However, letting this step go or not taking this step seriously is why so many businesses fail.

Everyone wants immediate gratification. They want clients right now. But the truth of the matter is that usually when people reach out to you the first time, they are researching. So, stay in front of them. Be top-of-mind awareness, stay in the forefront of your client's mind.

Formulating the Funnel

Once people know that you're an authority figure, that's when they'll listen. But to get to that point, you have to bring them along a "funnel." For example, when I wrote my first book, people weren't that interested in reading it until they saw my videos and realized, "Wow, she knows what she's talking about." Here's the funnel strategy for my coaching business to show you how a funnel works.

> *Once people know that you're an authority figure, that's when they'll listen. But to get to that point, you have to bring them along a "funnel."*

It starts by doing a ton of free video content, getting the videos out there, and getting people to know me, to like me and trust me. This begins to establish myself, not just as an expert, but as the authority figure. Once they see me as the authority, they do more research on me, right? When they do, they find my books because we were pointing the books towards them. As soon as they've seen the videos, we re-target them to the book funnel.

They go through the book funnel then they purchase my book. Once they read my book, they realize that, "Wow! She *really* knows what she's talking about!" We do have upsell offers as well. Once they purchase the book, they're asked if they want to buy the audio, and then they are prompted to join the 30-Day Challenge. (Check out the 30-Day Challenge at http://www.theultimatemarketingplaybook.com/member.) Once they get the book and read it, they continue to stalk and to watch me. Then we re-target them, create lookalike audiences and take them from the book funnel into the high-ticket coaching application.

And here's what's most important: The only reason that I ever got them from point A to point B to point C—from watching the videos, to purchasing the book, to getting into my high ticket funnel application, and finally becoming a client—is because I established myself as the authority figure in that subject matter from the very beginning with everything I did. That's why they know they should listen to me. Now, people will never listen to you until they know you're the authority, the only way they know you're the authority is by producing really good, valuable content. You produce content via creating videos, putting information on your blog, on your website, on YouTube, on Instagram, and wherever else makes sense so that they see you.

As another example, here's how that funnel works in my real estate business. We treat every precious lead that comes in like gold. Whenever a buyer contacts me through a site like Zillow or Trulia, we automatically send them a buyer's guide through our CRM (customer relationship management system). When a seller makes initial contact, we send them a seller's guide. These are not just the cheesy, generic seller's or buyer's guides. These guides are current and relevant, and changed every season to reflect market data and trends. We continue to follow up by email, sending them videos with valuable information that applies to their real estate market. We even deliver a great neighborhood guide to their front door! We also send out a video thanking them for contacting us and letting them know one of our associates will contact them shortly to answer any questions they might have.

Sarah Petty is a coach who specializes in helping photographers have profitable businesses. When someone has connected via her landing page and seen some of her free video tutorials, she starts by offering a $49 challenge to generate more business using certain tips like using print rather than digital photos to make more money. Next, she introduces them to an 8-week online course, then higher levels of coaching. The key is that she's given them something of value and asked for nothing in return. (By now, this theme should sound familiar!) Whether they become a client right then or not, they'll remember her because of the value she gave.

In both of my businesses, we have a company policy of a minimum of 7-9 touches. According to a recent study, **text messages** are the best method of communication because 93% of all text messages get answered within five minutes. For example, we'll send a text letting them know we've sent them an e-mail with information they can use, or a text asking if there is anything we can do to assist them. Sending a video text message or video e-mail is an excellent way to develop rapport and make a connection. Stand out, be different, show effort!!

> *According to a recent study, **text messages** are the best method of communication because 93% of all text messages get answered within five minutes.*

When I broke into the coaching industry there was another coach who specializes in real estate which is where I started my coaching. He's been coaching for several years. Finally, he approached me and said, "What the heck are you doing? You just, all of a sudden, came out of nowhere!" (However, there are no overnight success stories. I shed a lot of blood, sweat and tears behind the scenes). I was able to get a Four "2 Comma Club" awards from Click Funnels, which is an award that shows you did a million dollars in revenue with each of the four Digital Marketing Funnels. Though he'd been doing it for several years, he was shocked that I was able to make a mark in the coaching industry so quickly. You can grab a free two week trail of ClickFunnels by going to www.KristaMashore.com/ClickFunnels. Although, I don't think you should do this now, you should wait until you've read the entire book and are ready to take advantage of the free two-week trial.

So, get creative in your business and with your funnel. Once you've given them some valuable content and they've expressed some interest by giving you contact information, how can you keep them engaged? What else can you bring to them? What can you offer them that is helpful and establishes you as the authority? It's important to figure out your strategy so that it's **automatic**, you're prepared, and you know what path you're leading them on. Your funnel may change over time as you get new ideas. It doesn't have to be perfect. The important thing is to start with *something* and not just sit on it! Action is key.

A Peek Behind the Curtain

Back office activity may not seem exciting enough to impress a potential client—*unless* what you've got going behind the scenes shows the incredible value you'll be providing. Behind the Scenes is a lot more than just administration or shuffling paperwork. To create and maintain a healthy team environment, I highly suggest you read Dale Carnegie's book, *How to Win Friends and Influence People*. I listened to the audio book recently, then sent a copy to my entire staff and told them it was mandatory for them to listen to it or read it. Once they complete the book, I'll give them each $100.00. Why? Because the author is a genius, and I want to make sure my staff and I use the wisdom in this book as the basis for how we treat each and every person we interact with. (While my dad was proofing this, he asked if I'd give him $100.00 to read the book. Yes, Dad, it can help everyone!)

Everything my office staff does is focused on giving epic service. We treat our clients the way they'd be treated in a luxury hotel. We fulfill needs they didn't even know they had. We capture every lead and follow up as if they are the perfect person for our product, or that they'll be our next awesome student. We focus on being proactive, not waiting until a deal gets shaky, but spotting potential bumps in the road long before they appear.

The systems we have in place and the technology we've adopted allow us to do all of this. After someone becomes a client or student, we treat them like their doctor's office would treat them, with reminders the day before every appointment or deadline via text and email. This doesn't have to be tedious and time consuming. Software can do this easily and generate reminders automatically once you enter the dates. Three days before any deadline, we send them reminders of the task and offer encouragement and our help, if needed. All of this is automated via software, so nothing drops through the cracks. It also saves us time.

The point here is that everyone on your team has to have the same commitment to excellence. Have you ever stopped using a service provider because dealing with their staff was such a hassle? Their bookkeeper has been cranky or the person answering the phone is rude? After all you've done to earn that client's trust, you don't want someone in your staff to sour the relationship you've built.

Conversion: Harvest the Crop You've Sown

After lead generation and lead nurturing, it's time for the conversion phase. We need to convert that lead and turn that lead into an actual client, someone who's working with us or someone who's buying our product. How do we convert them? What is your lead conversion process? How are you converting your leads now that they've been nurtured and they're ready to choose someone to work with?

First let me tell you that, if you've nurtured this lead appropriately and you gave them information, you gave them value and you helped them, converting them is going to be much, much easier, and almost automatic! Because if you start from the beginning and do it correctly, working your way through the sales cycle using the 9 Cs, and making sure that you're properly serving your client every single step of the way, it gets easier and easier to convert.

> *if you've nurtured this lead appropriately and you gave them information, you gave them value and you helped them, converting them is going to be much, much easier, and almost automatic!*

With prior stages, you've connected with them and they trust you. You've also shown them that you understand their general pain points, goals and issues and can help with those pain points, goals and issues. You've established yourself as an authority and a valuable resource. The conversion stage is when you discover their unique *specific* pain points, goals and issues, and you show them very specifically how you can help them.

For example, you may have established that you understand the stress of being in debt and you know about how to help people out of debt. During conversion, you find out that your potential client has $24,000 in credit card debt, owes the IRS $1,500 and has a student loan of $32,000. Your job during the conversion stage is to be clear on how specifically you can help them with those debts.

Keep in mind, conversion is never about dazzling them with how terrific you are. You aren't focused on yourself but on them. You're NOT applying pressure or trying to scare them into working with you. That approach might get you a client in the short run, but your work with them will be miserable for both of you.

What's your conversion process? Whether it's in person, on phone or even via text, are you asking the right questions? Are you helping them understand specifically how you can help them? Are you helping them see that you are the best resource to fix that problem in a way that serves them? Are you helping the become aware of problems they didn't know they actually had. Are you making sure they realize you are the solution to those problems they weren't even aware they had? Having a plan for conversion makes it much simpler.

Let's look at some examples:

For loan officer Debbi Galvan, the conversion process happens when she talks to the potential borrower about their loan pre-approval. She has already run the numbers and done as much due diligence as she can at this stage, so she's pretty confident about the terms, type and amount of loan the client can expect at the end of the day. "It's really important at this stage to explain why this is their most likely scenario. They may have heard that their neighbor with tons of cash and perfect credit got some screaming hot interest rate or amazing terms that they just can't get. It's very sensitive for people. So, I take a lot of time to explain it all and to emphasize that I'm basing everything on my 20+ years of experience. Someone else may promise them a better deal, but at the very end of the transaction, they will likely not get what they were promised."

In my real estate business, the listing appointment is my point of conversion, though by this point, 99% of clients are already on board. Still, I bring a slew of facts and information to show them exactly what I'll be doing for them regarding marketing, negotiating, getting their home ready, etc. etc. I don't just show up, talk off the cuff and ask them to sign on the dotted line. I'm very clear about the exact service I intend to deliver. I find out what is most important to them in this sale, whether it's to sell by a certain date or get a certain amount out of the sale. And I'm also very realistic with them about their expectations, whether their timeframes and the price they want for their home is realistic.

For my coaching clients, we give, give, give. They've received a free eBook, watched a slew of videos, and gone through a very detailed process prior to making the decision to actually join one of my coaching programs. Typically, we have a preliminary appointment to go over their strengths and weaknesses and determine what program would be the best fit. Then we have a customer success coach meet with them to assess their needs, make further recommendations as to how we can help them and determine if we are even a good fit at all. The client knows we care and have their best interest at heart. We aren't just concerned about the sale. Sometimes we decline a potential client because we feel the program isn't right for them or right for them at this point in time based on what's going on in their lives.

Financial planner Carol Van Bruggen asks clients for financial information prior to their first meeting so she is prepared. Then that first meeting is all about getting clear on the client's goals, priorities and concerns. With that information, she can offer some possible avenues to reach those goals. She can tell them how long it should take to get where they want to be and ways to mitigate specific areas they're worried about.

Glenn Hoffman of Discovery Bay Insurance Services gets 100% of his business from referrals, so prospective clients already know they want to use his services. Still, he takes the time to explain how his company works and what they can expect from him. He also digs to find out what his new client really needs in the way of insurance versus what they may think they need. Based on his experience, he knows that sometimes they need more insurance, and sometimes they actually need less or a different type of policy. If his recommendations are different than what they had assumed, he takes the time to educate them.

Dance studio owner Nina Koch spends a lot of time talking to the parents of potential students during conversion. "This is a very emotional business. The parents are entrusting the most precious things in their lives to you. There can also be a lot of ego involved where a parent wants certain results for their child. So, I spend a lot of time emphasizing that it's the journey, not the result, that is the biggest benefit for the child, and that every child is unique and progresses at their own pace. This is often when I find out that this parent's expectations are not a fit for the culture we promote at our dance studio."

Nina makes a good point. The conversion stage is also usually the time when you decide whether you really want to work with that client. In my real estate business, if a client insists that I list the house for more than I know it's worth, I politely tell them I won't take the listing because I know I can't meet their expectation. In our coaching business we won't take anyone who gives us warning signs that they are looking for a magic pill and won't put in the

Work. And, of course, our "No A-Hole Policy" is always in effect.

For attorney Carol Delzer, if the divorcing couple is at each other's throats, each making impossible demands and seeking revenge, she politely tells them that divorce mediation may not be appropriate for them. As loan officers, Tracie Schmidt, Debbi Galvan and Tiffany Rose all agree that if a potential borrower lies or wants to fudge their financials to get a loan, they let that client know that will not work with them. (More on this in Chapter Nine). Insurance broker Glenn Hoffman will not work with clients who try to lie about their health or their business to get insurance, which often becomes apparent during his first interaction.

If you really pay attention during the conversion phase, you'll often be able to catch some red flags and avoid a lot of hassle down the road. And if you've done a good job with all the prior stages, conversion is easy!

> *If you really pay attention during the conversion phase, you'll often be able to catch some red flags and avoid a lot of hassle down the road.*

CHAPTER SEVEN

FULFILLMENT AND DELIVERY

So, you've done the work and have landed your client. Woo hoo! Now, how do you make sure that you give them the very best fulfillment process? Fulfillment is when you actually are delivering to them your services and they are working with you. Do not mess up here. Every phase of the sales cycle is essential but messing up this stage will put you out of business faster than any other stage!

When I was focused on real estate, I rarely discounted my commissions and I even charged a higher commission than the normal going rate. Did my clients squawk about the higher commission? Sometimes, but most often, they could see how much more value I provide compared to the average agent. I basically set a new standard of what it means to be a Realtor® in our area through the marketing I did for each property and the customer service I provided. Result? My clients were happier, and I sold their homes quicker and for more money than other agents could have gotten them.

For my coaching and training, I charge pretty high fees. Do my training and coaching clients complain? Nope. Because they can see in every step of their interactions with me and my staff that they are being taken care of and given valuable training that will truly make a difference in their lives. We make sure they get the results they come to us for. We don't just throw a bunch of information at them and call it good. We really care that they succeed, and it shows in everything we do.

We continue to give more support and value at every phase of their journey. We do things to show them that we care. I send gifts throughout their interaction with me, making sure they know that they weren't just important prior to becoming a client. They are still very important. For example, when we do live events (called summits), my students come to my personal home office from around the country and we treat them like kings and queens. My whole team shows up for the summit and bonds with them. We feed them incredible food and give them more gifts. They get one-on-one interaction with me and various team members. We make sure they know they are family to us. We are there to truly serve them!

People come to me because they recognize the difference between what I'm doing and what others do. Clients deserve that, they should expect it, and they get it from me. They see the value in what I do, and your clients should see it in what you do.

As a professional or business, whether you're an architect, a loan officer or an attorney, your services will not come cheap. You need to go above and beyond and *show* your clients the value you're providing to make sure they end up with the best result. The more you do that, the more your clients are going to boast about you and appreciate you. If you ever find yourself feeling uncomfortable about what you're charging, it just might be because you are doing what every other professional in your field is doing. You're just doing "the job" and not creating amazing service. You need to be different. You need to be better. And that means in *everything* you do.

> *If you ever find yourself feeling uncomfortable about what you're charging, it just might be because you are doing what every other professional in your field is doing.*

For example, Glenn Hoffman talks about how he deals with any of his clients who file an insurance claim. "Most agents today will not take the risk of getting involved with a claim. They will give the client what I call '1 800 Good Luck.' The client ends up going into some automated claim system and that agent never gets involved. We take the approach of, it's easy to do the sale and collect a commission. But where we shine is in the service that follows that sale. We will get involved, circumvent the system, and put our reputation on the line to make sure that the product we sold our client is performing the way we promised it would. We're at the table with them all the way through the process."

You want your clients to be so thrilled by your service that they are boasting about you even before they've finished with whatever service you offer.

So, what is your fulfillment and delivery process? What are you doing to ensure that they are just wowed by your services? It doesn't matter if they are the biggest client you've ever gotten or the smallest, whether the client signs a ten-year contract or is a one-off. You want them to be wowed by their experience with you. In fact, everyone we interviewed for this book said the same thing: It doesn't matter how big or small your client is. You treat them as if they are the most important client you've got. I highly recommend the book from Joey Coleman, *Never Lose a Customer Again*.

If you're wondering what amazing service would look like, here are some basic things to think about:

1. What does the average person in your business or profession do and how can you do it better?
2. What systems and support do you need so nothing ever falls through the cracks?
3. How can you let your clients know all you are doing for them and understand the incredible value you bring?

One strategy is to think about every phase of the interaction clients have with you. What can you do to make sure they feel supported and valued during each phase? For example, in my coaching business, when people first join, we send them a welcome package. It has the manual in it, a t-shirt, mouse pad, pens, stickers etc. We let them know how happy we are to have them. Then after one month, I personally call them to see how they are doing and give them encouragement. You would be amazed at how surprised they are to hear from me. Then at about month three, we send them a box of chocolates, with a note that says "Life is not like a box of chocolates. You were meant to be in our program." And then at month five we send them a branded sweatshirt. We didn't do all of this in the beginning. But as the company evolved, we continued to do more and more to show our clients how much we care about them not just before the sale, but *after* the sale!

Be the Ritz, Not Motel Six

If you've been in your business or profession for any length of time, you pretty much know what others in your profession do for their clients and customers. The question to ask is not "What's the least I can do to be adequate?" but "What more can I do?" "How can I serve more?"

Again, Glenn Hoffman of Discovery Bay Insurance Services is an awesome example of this. "After hours, if a client has a catastrophic loss, they have my cell phone they can call me. I tell them, 'You can call me. You call me at two o'clock in the morning, I'm gonna be asleep. But the phone is on my nightstand next to the bed. I will listen to that voicemail and if it's an urgent matter I will return your call, and I'll be in my car and I'll come see you that night if you need me.'"

This is not an empty promise. Glenn got a call one night from a couple who had just moved into their dream house and they were new to the area. The clients' dream house was on fire! Glenn threw on a baseball cap and drove over. The wife told him that everything they owned, including their wallets, were inside the house. They had absolutely nothing. "I already had my team at home with laptops open, filing the claim and working with the adjusters. We had a check overnighted to the clients the following morning, so they had money right away." Glenn also put them up in an in-law's quarters he had in his own home downstairs. "I just couldn't see putting them in a hotel when I had the ability to put them up. They stayed until their home was rebuilt and we became lifelong friends." And that, folks, is going above and beyond.

Above and beyond service doesn't always have to look that dramatic. My student Tracie Schmidt says, "As a loan officer, you can play an important part in the negotiations. I don't know a lot of loan officers who do this, but when I have a buyer who submits an offer on a home and there's multiple offers on that home, I find it's really important to call the listing agent. I introduce myself and go through all the strengths of the client's profile. I take that extra step to help my client stand out versus other clients and get the home they want."

Never Hesitate to Communicate

For most professions, it's important that your clients get ongoing communication. They need to know what you're doing for them and how it's progressing. Have you ever hired someone to do a job for you and at some point in the process, they've just ghosted you? A friend of mine once hired an architect. She met with him, paid him a retainer then didn't hear a peep from him for three weeks! Finally, she tracked him down and asked what was going on. "Oh, I had to put it aside for a rush job. I plan to get back on it and have it done in the next month." My friend wasn't in a big hurry, but it still grated on her. She never used him again or referred him even though his work was decent.

Honestly, I'd give many service professionals a C minus when it comes to client communication. It's as if they think, "Hey, I know what I'm doing. They don't need to know about it. I've got it covered." NOT GOOD! Also, be mindful to ask what type of communication they like best. Some clients prefer email, some text, some phone calls. Try to communicate with them in the manner that they are more likely to respond to.

Make sure your clients understand the process, whatever it is. To me, real estate is second nature, so it took me a while to understand that communicating isn't just telling my clients about the process. It's taking the time to make sure they understand it. I talk fast, which is okay, but I needed to learn to speak slowly enough so people can keep up with me. And I had to break it all down and explain the process like I did when I was teaching third graders. Not that my clients aren't smart, but they don't know what I know.

After creating all of the courses for my coaching business, I learned through further study that people learn better in smaller chunks. I ended up redoing my entire training to meet the needs of my students and tried to keep each training under seven minutes. We also realized that clients needed more support and accountability. So, we hired success coaches and accountability coaches. We added more trainings and drop-in office hours. Yes, this cost me a LOT more money. And honestly, at that time, the company wasn't ready financially to spend that kind of money. But we did it anyway. I knew it would pay off, because a happy client is a worth more than gold. And an unhappy client can cost you a fortune!

Every profession has its own lingo and its own way of doing things, and it changes constantly. For many professionals, clients deal with them infrequently or maybe only once. How often is someone going to come to you to handle their divorce? (Hopefully, not that often!) How many times will they need you to design their landscaping or coach their company through a merger? If I needed an electrician, I wouldn't have a clue about what that electrician needed to do. But if someone broke it down step by step, really took the time and articulated it so I could understand, I would be able to get it. And I would appreciate the time they took to explain it to me—and definitely feel better about the bill they handed me at the end!

I create videos for my clients to remind them of what's expected during every phase, whether it's in my coaching program or my real estate business because they forget what I've told them. We're often so caught up in doing our jobs, we forget that what comes so easily to us isn't that easy for them. Often, they will smile and nod, but once they walk out that door, the questions start flowing. They forget or didn't quite understand the terminology. They are bombarded with a lot of information all at once. They feel a certain amount of anxiety about the whole process.

Have you ever gone into a doctor's office where you're given a serious diagnosis of some kind? Even if it isn't life-threatening, your brain is so busy trying to absorb what it means to your life that you miss 80% of what the doctor tells you about it. If your doctor is good and breaks it down, you might think you understand. But as soon as you hit home and someone asks you about it, you realize that you don't fully understand what the doctor said or what comes next. It's the same with our clients.

I recently went with one of my best friends who was diagnosed with breast cancer to appointments with her doctors. She was meeting with a medical team to find out what her options were. Her husband was with her and she was beyond stressed and scared. It all happened so quickly. My friends are both incredibly smart. My friend's husband is a teacher and she is a Director of Human Resources for one of the largest school districts. When we walked out of that meeting, both she and her husband had misunderstood most of what they were told. Though I was worried for my friend, my emotions weren't as heightened as theirs. I was on alert and knew I had to listen carefully and take notes. I was able to clarify what the doctors had said.

When someone comes to you for your professional service, they do it because they don't know what you know or how to do what you do. They may have never been through the process before. They don't know what to expect from you or—and this can be deadly—they have expectations that are totally unrealistic.

Say someone comes to you for a chiropractic adjustment with the mistaken idea that their issue can be handled in one session. Or someone comes to you to handle their bankruptcy thinking they just have to fill out some paperwork and it's done. What if they think you'll be able to crank out the design for their dream house in two weeks and fit 4,000 square feet of space into an 1800 square foot home? Or that a simple eye lift will make them look forty years younger. Their expectations are based on what they don't know. If you don't tell them off the bat what they can expect from you, they'll be not only impossible to deal with but extremely unhappy at the end of the day.

> *If you don't tell them off the bat what they can expect from you, they'll be not only impossible to deal with but extremely unhappy at the end of the day.*

Think about your process and what your clients may not know about it. Maybe it's how expensive it will be, how much time it will take, or how much they'll need to participate. Maybe it has to do with terminology or results they can expect. Take the time to really put yourself in your client's shoes and remember what you didn't know before you knew all you know now. Remember back to what other clients have questioned or misunderstood. Then figure out a way to present good information to them.

Some professionals create written pieces to explain their process and what a client can expect. I've done videos because it adds the personal touch that everyone appreciates. In my real estate business, I actually send potential clients a series of short videos explaining each part of the process and what they can expect even before meeting with them. During the process, I send email videos to keep them informed of where we are in the process.

Carol Delzer, the divorce mediator in Sacramento, gives her book on divorce mediation, *Divorce Made Easy*, to her clients. It gives them pointers not only on the legal process but also the emotional roller coaster they can expect. Financial planner Carol Van Bruggen created a checklist for her clients who have had a death in the family. Obviously, someone who has just lost a loved one is not in the best shape to take in information. So, she laid out exactly what they need to do and all the documents they need to find. She put it in a step by step, easy to understand brochure that they can take home. Then she's available to answer any questions they may still have.

You could write up something or could create a Power Point presentation. You can present the information in person but that takes a lot of time and is probably not the best use of your time. If you chose to use videos, which I highly recommend, remember these video emails can be either standardized, made once then re-used or, if they are specific to one client, they can be made quickly using your laptop camera. Whatever you choose to do, do it well.

This also includes explaining potential bumps along the way. In my coaching business, I've noticed that there's a specific time at about 90 days into the program when many of my clients hit a wall. They've done the work, but they aren't yet seeing the results they want. They get discouraged and feel like giving up. However, I know that they are just on the verge of breaking through because I've seen it time and time again. But they don't know that.

So, I've learned to warn them up front. I tell them, "This isn't going to happen overnight. You may not see any results for the first three months. You may get discouraged that you don't have instant results. But keep going and know that your success is just around the next corner." With this information and reassurance, they keep moving forward—and it *does* happen for them!

For my real estate business, I have one video called *Seller Beware* that warns them about all the weird things that happen when agents start showing their house: People won't show up for their appointment. They'll use your bathroom and leave it messy. They'll lock the door you normally enter and leave closet doors and cupboards open.

In communicating with clients, one of the most important lessons you can learn is how to have difficult conversations. In other words, how to deliver or talk about "bad news." One of Tiffany Rose's biggest beefs about loan officers is that they often avoid these conversations. "It's not uncommon that a client calls in a panic because your assistant just sent a message that there's an issue with their loan or the loan has been denied. What I see too often is a loan officer who just texts back saying, 'Got your message. I'm working on it. I'll call you later.' But they never call. They just ghost them! Maybe they haven't been in the business long and they're scared. But that is the absolute worst thing you can do."

You simply have to face difficulties and conflict. This is true in all industries: The opposing side reneged on the settlement agreement. Their daughter didn't get the lead in the dance recital. Someone else outbid them on their dream house. The kitchen design they want came in costing twice as much as their budget. As Tiffany puts it, "Just pick up the darn phone. If a client's pants are on fire and they're mad or upset, deal with them. Be emotionally aware and empathetic. Talk them out of their tree. Avoiding them and letting the situation simmer is the worst strategy ever."

Often, you can head off problems before they happen by being proactive. As part of her fulfillment process, Tiffany contacts every client 30 days after a close to make sure they got their mortgage statements. "People get busy with life, especially after moving and you'd be surprised how many don't see the mortgage statement come in, so they don't pay in their first month! It's much better to be proactive than to have an unhappy client who is embarrassed because they missed their first loan payment."

A friend of mine told me about going to an acupuncturist for the first time. He got poked with needles and was given a bunch of nasty herbs to take over the next week. A couple of days later, someone from the acupuncturist's office called just to see how my friend was doing and to see if he had any questions. Think about it: How would you feel if your chiropractor, yoga instructor, doctor or therapist called or shot you a quick note just to follow up and see how you're doing? Wouldn't you feel special? Wouldn't you tell your friends about that professional?

Another friend had her eight-year old son in local martial arts classes. She told me that every month or so, one of her son's instructor's would send her son a hand-written postcard that said, "I noticed you were working really hard last week" or "I can tell you're really paying attention in class." It not only encouraged her son but let her know how much the school and its instructors cared about each student.

Clients totally appreciate updates on whatever you're doing for them, whether it's processing their loan, creating the marketing campaign or planning their event. Again, it's about showing your value as well as keeping in touch. Keeping your client informed and showing them that you are doing everything you can takes the heat off.

Think about your own business. What do your clients need to know? What do they *want* to know? How can you set their expectations? What problems or blips might they encounter?

Flawless Fulfillment

In professional services, tracking the process, deadlines and progress in what's happening is often a critical piece of the work. I've always used an automated customer tracking system as soon as the fulfillment piece begins. Someone else might use an Excel spreadsheet just as effectively if their process is simpler. Tracking systems are there to track everything, where it is in the process and where it should be, what needs to happen before what, whose responsibility it is and exactly when and how you'll all check in with other people involved and with the client.

Tiffany Rose makes reviewing her tracking system a daily ritual for herself and her staff. They don't just check in every few days. They use it to be proactive and communicate to everyone concerned about upcoming deadlines. They use it to make sure they are ahead of the curve when it comes to escrow so, at least from their side, there will be no unpleasant surprises at the close.

And it doesn't stop for Tiffany when the loan closes. "Every time a loan closes, a thank you card goes out to the listing agent and buyer's agent and the client. We also send our clients closing gifts. But if you're just new in the business and can't afford closing gifts, at least send a thank you card. Be sure to send a handwritten, not just an email or a text."

Being clear on deadlines and timeframes with your client can save a ton of anxiety and angst. Attorney Carol Delzer says, "I always give my clients the dates and timeframes for when their paperwork will be done and filed. This not only gives them a sense of certainty, but it gets this deadline on my calendar. I make that commitment to deliver on the date I said I would." She adds, "Whenever you find yourself in crisis mode, that you feel behind or know that things are falling through the cracks, trust me,

> *"Whenever you find yourself in crisis mode, that you feel behind or know that things are falling through the cracks, trust me, you've got an unhappy client somewhere even if they haven't expressed it yet."*

you've got an unhappy client somewhere even if they haven't expressed it yet."

About the #*!#! Phones

Okay, so what about your system for answering the phones? Honestly, isn't one of the biggest frustrations of modern life the Black Hole of automated voice mail systems? You punch this number then the next number and somehow end up waiting on hold listening to cheesy music for twenty minutes only to find out you've got the wrong person! Getting a good system in place for taking client calls is golden. Having a rotten and frustrating phone system in place is deadly. Depending on your business, there are different ways to handle phones.

Attorney Carol Delzer says that the number one complaint the State Bar hears about attorneys is that *they don't return phone calls.* At her office during office hours, Carol does not have voice mail. The call is sent through to one of her assistants who then sets up a phone appointment for the caller within 48 hours. This is helpful in many ways: 1) Carol isn't disrupted constantly during the day so can get her work done. 2) She has the opportunity to prepare for the caller by pulling their file, so the call is more efficient. 3) Her client knows exactly when they will get to speak with her and, because it's an appointment, they know they will be billed. 4) There is no back and forth of missed calls and connections or garbled messages. "I've never had a complaint and clients know that they're getting my best."

In his insurance business, Glenn Hoffman also avoids voicemail as much as possible. "I never want a client in the event of a loss or when they're frustrated to go to voicemail. We have four lines and four staff members in the office. However, if all four of us are on the phone, we can't grab that call. It goes to voicemail but whoever is free first will return that call. We also don't close for lunch. I stagger the lunch hour in the office, so the office remains open. I promise the clients that anytime they call Monday through Friday from 8:00 to 5:00, they're gonna get a live voice." Glenn also gives his clients his private cell phone for after-hours emergencies. "I tell all my clients, 'In an emergency, you can call me.' In the course of 13 years, I've had three or four events that were middle of the night emergencies. And I've never had a client abuse that offer."

Financial planner Carol Van Bruggen does use voicemail but makes sure that she or one of her assistants gets back to the caller that same day. She says, "I think one thing that we do differently is that we take every call seriously. Even if they start the message with 'I was just wondering about. . .' the fact that they bothered to call means that something is going on and it's important to them."

Other professionals I know set up specific hours when they return phone calls (and emails). They let their clients know their phone schedule and have it on their voice message: "If you call before 3:00, I will return your call between 3:00 and 5:00 that same day. Unless it is an emergency, I'll return calls received after 3:00 the following day." This is especially helpful if you are a one-person operation.

Time to Toot Your Horn!

Often the work we do as service professionals is under the radar. The client sees results but isn't aware of how we helped get them there. I think that's a mistake. We want them to be clear on the value we provided. This is easier in some businesses or professions than others. For example, in my real estate business, I can keep them informed about all the ads we're running for them, the number of showings their house is getting, how many views we've had on our social media posts, how many hours of watch time, and how many postings we've done for them or text blasts.

In something like coaching or therapy, it's trickier but still possible. I like to remind my coaching clients how far they've come. "When we started together, you felt stuck and didn't know which way to turn. Now you're all fired up about putting together your new personal training business. You're developing a following on Facebook and you've already got three clients. Congratulations!"

As a plastic surgeon or a chiropractor, you might want to take before and after photos. As an architect or landscape designer, you can take before, after and during photos. As a financial planner, you can give them "snapshots" of their finances along the way until they reach their goals.

Why is this important? In my real estate business for example, clients are excited and refer other people to me even before we've sold their home. They are clear about all the efforts we are making on their behalf and they trust that I know what I'm doing. If, for some reason, the house isn't selling as quickly as they'd hoped, they know it is not because we are not doing everything we can. This applies to your profession as well.

The Benefits of Great Fulfillment

Insurance broker Glenn Hoffman says, "I still have some of our very first clients, some of them I wrote their first policy 30 plus years ago. It takes time and energy. And consistent, persistent behavior to always do what you promise to do. To always go above and beyond for my clients. By doing all of this, my business is now 100% referral."

Carol Van Bruggen of Foord, Van Bruggen and Pajak Financial Services agrees. "When I first got in the business, my mentor Dusty Miller told me, "Always do your very best for clients. Never cut corners. Never even squeak around ethical issues. Do what's right and not what's self-serving. Remember what you say you're going to do and do it. And if you do all this, and hang in there, your business will become easier and easier.' I didn't really believe him at the time, but I followed his advice. And he was 100% correct. All my business is by referral now."

Loan officer Debbi Galvan is also adamant about excellent delivery. One Realtor® was so impressed with her service that she referred her to another Realtor® friend. Between both of them, she's now done loans for everybody in their family. For one of them, she's handled loans for all three of her kids. The interesting thing is that the first Realtor® wasn't doing that much business at the time she met Debbi. She had approached Debbi with a client who was buying in a new subdivision. Debbi told them that, though she'd love to be their lender, she knew that the builder's lender would be able to kick in $10,000 for closing costs. She steered them back to the builder because she knew the builder could give the borrowers a better deal. Debbi also told them to call her if they needed anything explained as they went through the process. This Realtor® never forgot Debbi's honesty and willingness to help, and she became totally loyal to Debbi as her own business grew. *That's* the kind of service you want to provide.

One of the ways to ensure that clients do not have buyer's remorse is to give them an exceptional fulfillment process. You are delivering such high value, such high customer service. You are organized. You are keeping them informed. You're doing everything that you said that you would and more. Does that make sense? You want to make sure that you give them such a great experience that they can't help but tell all of their friends. That is why having an amazing fulfillment and delivery process is so, so important.

Take the Next Step

1. *Make a list of all the valuable things you do for your clients already. Identify any holes you see in how you're working with clients today. How can you improve and make any deficiencies better?*
2. *Write down 3 ideas from this chapter and schedule a time to implement them in your own business.*

CHAPTER EIGHT

THE THREE R'S: REFER, RETAIN, RESELL

The last three stages, which also are very important, are the three R's; refer, retain, and resell. How do you make sure that they refer you? How do you make sure that you retain that client after your work with them is done and that they'll always come back? And if you have other offerings beyond the first services they used, how do you make sure that they will come to you for those as well?

We all think that our clients love us and that they're never going to forget us, right? But this doesn't happen automatically. It takes some effort on your part. Do you know that it costs you seven times more money to obtain a new client than it does to keep an existing one? What does that tell us? It tells us that, while getting leads is important and easy, *retaining* the clients that we already have, making sure that they come back with us and that they want to work with us again is incredibly valuable in building a sustainable business.

In his book, *Never Lose a Customer Again: Turn Any Sale into Lifelong Loyalty in 100 Days*, Joey Coleman gives some really interesting statistics. He writes that just a 5% improvement in customer retention rates will yield a 25% to 100% increase in profits. He also says that according to marketing metrics, when selling to a new prospect you have a 5% to 20% chance of making the sale. But when you're selling to an existing customer, that probability skyrockets to 60% to 70%. What about client retention? According to Coleman's book, if a company has a 5% churn rate versus a 20%

churn rate, that improved retention will translate into a positive 280% increase in the company's valuation over a five-year period.

As Tiffany Rose says, "Of course I love the marketing and all of that. But my biggest asset is in my book of business and my past clients. I've adopted the 'by referral only mentality.' This means that you treat every client equally, no matter what size loan amount or where they live. You keep in contact with them and you show them you value them. It's not about the money. It's the customer experience that is so important to me. I love having the 'by referral only' attitude. It's not only more productive but I'm always getting new clients that I really want to have because they've been referred by my past clients." Tiffany says that now her efforts in marketing, advertising and social media is just icing on the cake.

> *I love having the 'by referral only' attitude. It's not only more productive but I'm always getting new clients that I really want to have because they've been referred by my past clients."*

Being Unforgettable

The key to refer, retain, resell is top of mind awareness, meaning your clients think of you and remember you. Just the other day, my husband and I were starting some work on our property. He said, "Babe, who was that guy that cut our trees? He was really good." This contractor had done work for us about four or five years before. I said, "I can't remember, babe. I can't remember who it was. But, yeah, he was terrific." How often has that happened to you, where someone provided amazing service but when you need them again, you can't remember their name? Or how many times have you worked with a particular service provider but when you need that service again, you don't even think of them? You had every intention to use that professional again, but "out of sight out of mind." With so much bombarding us every day, it's so easy to forget people who've provided good service for us.

To be honest, in the first ten years of my real estate business, I wasn't very good about keeping in touch with past clients and following up. I can't tell you how many times back then that I'd see a client, and they'd be so happy to see me. Then they'd say, "Oh, Krista, we bought a house. We're so excited." And I'd think, "What the heck?!?" I knew they loved working with me, but I didn't keep in touch with them. Now I understand that prior clients are assets that are way too precious to be treated like yesterday's newspaper! Not following up back then cost me a lot of business.

My father used to own a company in Tahoe, NV called Second Home Care that does monthly maintenance on vacation homes. He told me that if his clients didn't get an update from him *at least* once per month about their home and the specific maintenance his company performed for them, his company would lose thousands of dollars every year.

Out of Touch, Out of Mind

You can find literally thousands of ways to stay in touch with your clients so that they keep you in mind. I try to stay in front of my clients as much as possible in ways they'll appreciate, not ways that just annoy them. Some are digital, some face to face. With both, I have two rules: 1. Whatever you do, do it differently than everyone else is doing it. Be creative. Be innovative. Be different and give value. 2. Do it consistently. If you only plan to do it once or twice, don't bother doing it at all!

Here are some ways I stay in touch with my real estate clients:

1. The number one way to stay in touch is using social media and creating videos that provide value. With social media, you are showing up where they are. You can upload your contact list into Facebook to capture your past clients. When you do this consistently, you are staying top of mind awareness. Alex Mayer, one of my coaching clients, said that his referral business had increased by eight times just from consistently using

video and properly distributing them. Your past clients can't help but remember you when they continue to see you on social media. Even if they don't have a need for your services, they are reminded to refer you to those who may. This is the single BEST way to stay top of mind awareness. Social media is where most everyone is. Think about when you go out to dinner: When you look around the restaurant, you'll see half the people with their heads down looking at their phones (which actually is kinda sad, isn't it?). More often than not, they are on social media.

2. Holiday parties: Everyone does Christmas parties, so I do a Thanksgiving party with a pie give-away. At Christmas, I'll do an event where we serve hot chocolate and cookies, have Santa, a balloon maker, face painting and a jumpy house for the kids. I also encourage everyone to bring canned goods for the local food drive.

3. Holiday greetings: Rather than cards, I send out a blast text message wishing everyone Happy Holidays (93% of all text messages get opened within 5 minutes).

4. Client appreciation parties: I do one every year with food, a "casino" night with play money, and games with prizes.

5. BombBomb video emails: I send out generic Happy Birthday, Happy Anniversary, and Happy Anniversary on the sale or purchase of their house videos. Though the message is the same, their name shows up in the greeting, so it feels as if it was made just for them.

Different methods work for different businesses or professions. Financial planner Carol Van Bruggen hosts informational lunches with expert speakers. For example, when tax laws changed, she had a tax attorney and a tax accountant speak at the luncheon. Clients are encouraged to invite a friend.

Divorce mediator Carol Delzer focuses on the therapists and real estate agents who refer clients to her. "Twice a year, I send out 3,500 full-color postcards to them. My photo is on the front with some kind of clever saying or quote. A postcard is easy to send and more effective because they don't have to open it. And they look forward to the new message every time." She also sends them copies of her books on divorce and co-parenting and offers them additional free copies so they can lend it out to clients.

Tiffany Rose shoots out weekly informational emails to her client list. She'll also do Happy Thanksgiving and Happy Birthday emails that are all automated in her CRM. Many of her prior clients follow her on Facebook so she also does quick videos with valuable information to help stay in touch.

Keep in mind that other professionals who refer clients to you are "clients" also. Keep in touch by giving them something that makes their job easier. As a loan officer, if you get referrals from real estate agents, you could send them a step-by step guide to getting loan pre-approval that they can share with their clients. It makes the agent not only look smart but helps establish you as the authority that agent can trust. If you're a contractor who gets referrals from architects, you could send them a quick guide of typical renovations and cost ranges to share with their clients.

> *Keep in mind that other professionals who refer clients to you are "clients" also.*

Let me share a story about how important being top of mind is. Recently my husband and I built a home in Discovery Bay on deep water. We had to get all new blinds for the home. We loved our blind lady, she was absolutely amazing. However, after the "installation" of our blinds, she never kept in contact with us. I have been asked for a referral for blinds, and I couldn't give her information because I forgot not only her phone number, but her name and her company name. She hasn't kept in contact, stayed top of mind, or reached out to me in any way. No email, no Facebook presence, nothing. So… she's lost out of numerous referral opportunities.

To stay in touch, you can send out informational videos with quick tips. You can send past clients alerts about upcoming community events they'd enjoy. You can shoot out a BombBomb video email that just says, "Wishing you a great week!" The bottom line is that people want communication. They want a personal touch, and this applies to *every* type of business. That's how they'll remember you.

You can also send personalized video text messages. You can just use the video on your phone, or a service like BombBomb. (If you use, BombBomb be sure to say my name, we will both get a little extra something lol). I encourage my students to send ten video text messages every day to their sphere of influence, people they've recently met, friends of friends, people who like or comment on their posts, etc. Just look them up on social media, see what they've had happen that's cool in their life recently, press record and wish them well. Make it personal, don't ask for business, just recognize them. This goes a long way and people really enjoy it.

Perfecting the Process

I keep in contact with my previous clients *forever*. Obviously by now, I have a ton of prior clients and there's no way I can follow up manually. Everything is automated, so no one slips through the cracks. I touch base with my clients several times throughout the year in different ways. Again, the key is offering value to them, not just, "Hi, remember me? I'm still designing residential landscapes/ offering personal training/doing business consulting." CRM's (customer relationship management systems) now come in all price ranges. Get whatever you plan to do automated. And that means figuring out what you want to do and how often.

One of the systems Tiffany Rose uses is what she calls the "A, B, C's." She'll go through the alphabet two letters per week and personally contact prior clients whose names begin with those letters. "Within a year, you end up contacting them personally at least twice."

Refer

If you are doing an excellent job during the fulfillment stage, getting referrals happens organically. As insurance broker Glenn Hoffman says, "We've been persistent. We went from pounding the pavement and spending of thousands of dollars on marketing, direct mail advertising, getting involved with the organizations in our niche, putting ourselves out there and doing all those things to try to drive business to our front door. Fast forward to today with our relationships with folks like Krista and others in the community, and just living up to our promises over the years. We are now 100% referral-based."

You will *earn* your referrals as you go along. What's even more powerful is to *ask* for them. Too many businesses and professionals simply don't remember to ask. Think about it. When a client has just had a great experience with you and had great results from the work you

> *You will earn your referrals as you go along. What's even more powerful is to ask for them.*

did for them, that's when they're feeling all warm and fuzzy. If you've gone above and beyond, they want to give you something back. Simply saying, "Can you think of someone else that I could serve?" will get their brains working. "Hmmm. Who do I know?" Most of us send thank-you's after our work with clients is done, right? How about including that one small sentence, "Can you think of someone else I could serve?" Ask people once they've devoured that meal at your restaurant, to go online and give you a review on Yelp. It's that simple, just ask.

Tiffany Rose starts the process early. "I think loan agents and other professionals are afraid to ask for referrals. But it can be huge. I'll call up and say, 'Hey I'm glad you're so happy. Congratulations your loan is approved. And I know that this is going to be very smooth all the way through to close of escrow. By the way, can you think of three people that I can serve and help, even if they're not ready to buy right now? Maybe even someone who thinks it's impossible for them to buy. Can you think of anybody that I can serve?' If you get in the habit of doing that, you'll be amazed at the referrals you get."

Besides her other writing, writer Heather Estay does a lot of ghostwriting and usually has more business than she can handle, all from referral. But whenever the pipeline is looking slim, she'll shoot out an email to her favorite clients. "I've got some capacity right now. Can you think of anyone who could use my services?" She says, "I always get some good introductions to potential clients from this. Then I make especially sure that I do a great job for that person a client has introduced to me, knowing that how I show up for this new person reflects back on my client."

Glenn Hoffman agrees. "We've developed a network with real estate agents and mortgage agents. When folks like Krista have clients who need home insurance, they need to get it done in a timely way. My pledge to them is we will never slow an escrow. You may have many other issues that cause delays—credit, inspections, valuations—but our agency will never be a part of that. When Krista or another realtor or mortgage person comes to us for an evidence request, that is top priority for Christina in our office. Everything else is dropped and that's taken care of."

In real estate, when a transaction is over, I send a thank you video and ask for a referral and a testimonial. I've found this to be much more powerful than asking for a referral and testimonial by plain email.

Which brings me to testimonials: Ask for them! When people are looking for different services or when they are researching you, they will look you up on all those services that rate service providers. Yelp has most types of businesses and almost every business and profession has their own sites where people can leave comments and ratings. In real estate-related businesses, Zillow is a good source. For the legal profession, there's Lawyers.com. Do a Google search to find what works best for your industry. Once you know what sites are used, let your client know where to post their testimonial and give them the links to those sites. It will save them time and hassle and they're more likely to actually do it.

One site I use is called SoTellUs. I just love this site because it takes only minutes to use and it automatically spits out the review onto platforms like Google My Business, Yelp, Facebook and many others. Your clients can leave a written review or a video testimonial (I always encourage them to do a video, it's much more powerful and can be transcribed to use as a written testimonial as well). I always give away prizes and ask for referrals during parties and when I do large speaking events. I've gotten over 51 reviews in one day with the strategy that I use. If you'd like to learn more about the strategy that I use. Go to www.TheUltimateLeadGenPlaybook.com/member.

I also have an awesome relationship with SoTellUs because I refer them so often, so they give my referrals a massive discount. They cut their monthly fee in half and the waive the set up fee. You can get more information on that on the website listed above as well.

Resell

Not all services are natural resell opportunities. When you've completed the interior design of a client's home, you're pretty much done with that client until they move or decide to renovate. But many other businesses and professions have resell or upsell opportunities built in.

For a local restaurant or clothing store, you could offer a 20% off coupon for friends or family for the next 30 days when they bring in your receipt or mention your customers name. Don't be afraid to give discounts, if you've got a great product or service, you want "new" customers coming in, and old customers remembering how awesome your establishment, product or service is. Get more people through your doors buying your "stuff."

For Nina Koch, her dance studio clients have to be resold every fall. "The dance studio business tracks with the school calendar. All of our ongoing classes end in the summer. We offer summer workshops and programs but when September comes around, we need to get all of our students re-enrolled. We are very proactive but can't begin until August because people don't want to plan too far in advance. This year we did a texting campaign. We sent a simple text message to every single family who had not already registered for the fall. It simply said, 'Hi! Are you interested in dance classes again this fall?' We got a huge response. Then we took a very hands-on approach and, instead of telling them to go to our website to register, we continued the text conversation with, 'Great. This was the class that Sally was recommended for last year. Would you like me to register you?' if they said yes, we registered them on the spot." Hard to resist that, right?

When Carol Delzer completes a divorce mediation, obviously she doesn't try to sign her clients up for another divorce! But she has other attorneys who work for her with different specialties like Family Trusts or Wills. If she sees that her newly divorced clients might need these services, she offers to set them up with an informational interview with that other attorney.

Coaching and training services often have resell and upsell opportunities. Think about giving bonuses or creating new content that can add value to past students. We recently offered a huge discount for our two-year anniversary. We offered a discount on our monthly coaching if they paid an upfront one-time fee, and then we discounted the yearly fee by $800.00. We got a great response. Anytime we see something new and innovative in the market, we learn it, master it, and then offer it as a training. Reaching out to our past list is essential. We recently launched our podcast, and our list is what got us over two hundred 5-star reviews and thousands and thousands of downloads. Going back to people who have already pulled out their credit cards for you and getting them to rebuy, is much easier than getting new customers (as long as you have given them an amazing experience).

Just as in everything else you do, reselling is about service to your client. What other services could they really use? How else could you help them? It's not trying to sell them something they don't need.

Those are the three Rs. Once your client's work with you is complete, you've got to make sure that you're still top-of-mind awareness. You're still engaging them. You're still reaching out to them. You're holding up your hand and saying, "Hey, I'm still

> *Once your client's work with you is complete, you've got to make sure that you're still top-of-mind awareness.*

here. How can I serve you?" You're still adding value to them. You're not just saying, "Hey, give me a referral," or, "Use my product." You're making their life better, right?

To ensure that your business is not like the 95% of businesses that fail, implement and be consistent with the eight stages of a complete sales cycle. The cycle never ends. The goal is to continue to have people going through your cycle and come back to you when they have a need for your services. They can't do that if they don't remember and they're not going to do that if you don't give them an amazing experience.

And remember, each phase of the sales cycle is important as each phase feeds into the next, its line an infinity sign, never ending.

Take Action

1. *Review what you currently do to stay top of mind with your clients. Think of 3 new ideas you could implement.*
2. *Look at your current system of getting referrals and testimonials. What can you do differently to get more and more consistently?*
3. *What can you offer your clients as resell opportunities?*
4. *Go to www.TheUltimateMarketingPlaybook.com/member to learn more about how to get great testimonials.*

CHAPTER NINE

WORKING SMARTER, NOT HARDER

If you're reading a book like this, I doubt you're lazy. You probably work as hard or harder than your peers. Hard work is part of succeeding in any business, but the real key is to work *smart*. Too many people confuse being busy with being productive.

Use Technology for Efficiency and Impact

Many local businesses or professionals in the service industries do not operate with huge staffs, especially when they are starting out. Personally, I could not do all I do without automating a lot of my processes. As you start following the strategies I've laid out in this book to become a Community Market Leader in your field or business, you'll find that automating your processes is absolutely necessary for you too.

Let's talk about a couple of technologies that can make a tremendous difference as you build your business. The first I always recommend is a client relationship management (CRM) platform (yes these are important for restaurants, clothing stores, and service providers too.) For my businesses, I use Realvolve for Real Estate and Ontraport for coaching business, because they have all the features I love, they are easy to use and cost effective. You can research other CRM's out there and figure out which is best for you.

Your CRM, if used properly will become your new best friend! It will calendar your social media campaigns and your complete sales cycle so you can "set it and forget it." You'll set up aspects of it to capture leads from the landing page or website and take these leads through the lead nurturing process—sending out a series of emails, text messages, offers, informational videos. Down the road, the system will help you stay in touch with clients with holiday greetings, discounts and promotions, future offers, more informative videos, etc. The CRM will track and help you acknowledge clients' and customers' important dates, like birthdays, and anniversaries (it is a way to bring them back into your establishment.)

If you're a restaurant or brick and mortar, think about what you could offer to honor your customers. How can you get them back into your establishment? Maybe you give them a buy one get one on their birthday. Or you give them a free pizza, hat or shirt with the purchase of $20.00 or more (or you give it to them for free on their special day, that's what Denny's does.) Constantly be thinking about how to get your customers and clients back into your world. Don't focus on what you're giving away (meaning a loss), focus on what you're bringing in. Goodwill goes a long way, the more you give to your clients and customers, the MORE they are going to tell everyone.

By the way, here's how I do standard videos to be efficient: I make a really good, upbeat generic happy birthday video. Then when our CRM sends it out, the email subject line itself says, "Hi, John Doe. I just wanted to make sure I caught you on your special day." They click on the video and it's like a continuation of the greeting. So, even though it's generic, it feels personal. But, understand that doing personalized video where you say their name and truly make it personal, is always more powerful. So if you have the time or are starting out, I suggest you try to do that and make the video as personal as you can.

Every CRM these days can also help you track the processes during fulfillment while you're working with a client. In both my real estate and training business, we have specific protocols for everything we do. I now have teams who are responsible for different parts of our process with clients. We've loaded our CRM with our processes so it can track our activity and generate checklists to keep us on point. Everything is task-driven and we're very systematic about what specific activities happen during each phase of every marketing campaign, conversion, and fulfillment.

The CRM can alert you to start dates, deadlines and critical tasks that need to be completed before others can be done. It can keep notes of individual client progress and their next steps. If your client will need certain information from you during the stages of your fulfillment, your CRM can be set up to automatically know when to send that information.

Your CRM tracks each task and who is assigned to each task. It can send out reminders to both your team and your clients (and any outside party who needs to be informed) via text or email a few days before any appointment or deadline. When a task is completed, your CRM records it. The paperwork of your fulfillment process is also stored with your CRM for easy access.

The important thing to note here is that *anything* you do can be made simpler and more efficient by good use of technology. It keeps the team or a you as an individual organized, informed, and able to retrieve information quickly. Rather than having to remember and remind everybody about dead-

> *The important thing to note here is that* anything *you do can be made simpler and more efficient by good use of technology.*

lines, your CRM can send out texts to your client and team that say, "Loan docs due in 3 days" or "Update Facebook ad." And because everything is run through our CRM, if someone on my team gets sick or is on vacation, someone else can step in and know exactly what's been done and what they need to do next.

Think about all the time and mental energy this type of system can save you! Even if it's a stretch financially, if you don't have a good CRM, I highly recommend you get one and use one as soon as you can.

Rather than recreating the wheel every time, I also use a service to automate my marketing pieces. It has templates that my team can just fill in with appropriate information. Loan officer Tracie Schmidt uses a service to create marketing pieces for real estate agents she works with. "I use a program called Vista Reports that allows me to build flyers for real estate agents I work with and provide them marketing support for their listings. A lot of agents aren't all that creative so it's a huge value to them."

My CRM also interfaces with another technology I use, Bomb-Bomb. BombBomb sends out all of my video emails and tracks their open rates. It also has a feature that auto-detects the recipient's devices and connection speeds, then it sends the optimal video format to them. Once you set this interface up, it's another "set it and forget it" type of thing. The best thing is that BombBomb now has an advanced option to ensure you don't miss anything. It's super easy and mobile phone compatible which makes it convenient and ensures you'll use it.

This brings up an important point: You need to be tracking the traffic and effectiveness of your posts and emails. For example, if you send 100 emails, how many are really getting opened? Say, ten of them bounce for bad ad-

> *You need to be tracking the traffic and effectiveness of your posts and emails.*

dresses. Ninety get delivered and ten of those are opened. Then how many of those people take the next step? Your CRM should be able to tell you so you can tweak what you're doing to get better open and conversion rates. Our CRM can tell us who is opening and clicking through. This helps us focus on the correct target market and the information that is attractive to them.

One note about email: Be careful about becoming identified as a spammer. If you blast out too many emails, your email can get blocked as spam, and no-one will get your emails. We always try to get contacts on our lists to opt in, especially to our video market updates.

You can access other reports that will tell you how effective your ads and posts are like with Google analytics. Using analytics, we can tell if we need to change something to get more traffic, maybe by using a different photo or tweaking the wording.

For any contracts and documents needed during fulfillment, we use a combination of our CRM and Docusign which allows us to do digital signatures. The software allows us to easily get everything on the drive at the end of the fulfillment process, so the file is all in one easy-to-access place.

The point is to train yourself to think, "What technology is available to make each process better, smoother, more innovative and easier? What will help save you time so you can provide the service and do the work you really want to do?"

Get Support You Need

Even with the efficiencies of technology, as you start grasping what it really means to be Community Market Leader™, you'll probably think, "Yikes! That's a lot of work!" It is. And as you progress, though you can do a lot of it yourself, you are going to have to get some help and put some money into it.

Nina Koch found herself in that place very early in the process of building her dance studio, East County Performing Arts Center. "When I bought the studio, I was seven months pregnant then took the helm as owner with a three-week old baby. It was just me at the beginning. I was teaching classes and I was working the office. We jumped from 80 kids to 150 within three months, which was a huge jump for us. I realized really quickly that doing all the office work during the day, then teaching 20 plus hours in the evenings was not going to be stable for long." Nina knew she had to bring on help. "And I knew right away that I only wanted to hire people who were smarter, more creative, more educated than I was, and I've always been committed to doing that.

Nina realized that she needed help in two areas: She needed more dance instructors and she needed help on the business side. "Because I was a creative person, passionate and a really good dance teacher, when I chose to start my own school, my family just threw money at me. They thought I was a magical unicorn who could do no wrong. Nobody asked me if I had a business plan or a lawyer or an accountant or if I even knew how to balance a checkbook—which I didn't. I really went into this business 100% creative and passionate with very little business acumen or business knowledge. So I realized quickly that I needed to bring in help."

That is so true of a lot of service professionals! You got into your field because you love to design landscaping, or you want to help kids get into the college of their choice, or you love feeding people (god knows I do lol.) You love helping people secure their financial futures or you want to make sure people have awesome weddings. You didn't necessarily get into it for the Big Bucks. However, as Nina has learned, "No money, no mission." If you don't set your business up to be financially sustainable, you won't get to provide the service and make the impact you want with your profession.

> *If you don't set your business up to be financially sustainable, you won't get to provide the service and make the impact you want with your profession.*

Please remember, this is *your* business. You cannot expect to make a decent living without spending money to make money. All successful businesses have expenses. They allocate money for marketing, employee costs, and equipment. Any other businesses typically have a lot more expenses than you'll ever incur. The investment you make into your business will pay off, guaranteed. Keep in mind that you don't have to build up your support system all at once. Take it in steps.

Keep being innovative and unique, even on a shoestring budget. Then as you start to make money, it's time to set up a real marketing budget. I recommend a marketing budget that is 20% of your gross revenue. This may sound steep, but it will make so much more money for you as you move forward. Again, you have to be thinking like an entrepreneur. One article I read recently stated:

- Companies that grew 1-15% year over year spent an average of 16.5% of their revenue on marketing
- Companies that grew 16-30% year over year spent an average of 22% of their revenue on marketing

- Companies that grew 31-100+% year over year spent an average of 50.2% of their revenue on marketing[1]

Here's the truth about marketing budgets: The more that you spend the more you're going to make. Assuming you're marketing strategically, he who can market the most wins. He who can pay more for marketing will always beat out the next person because he or she is being seen more and are exposed more. You always have to ask yourself, "How big do I want to be? How quickly do I want to get there?" The more that you can market yourself to let your target audience know that you're the authority figure and the more you can spend on it, the quicker you're going to get to the next place. I always tell my students that marketing is leverage. When you have more leverage you don't have to have the most experience or be the smartest. When you have more leverage you will have more opportunity to win.

I'm still relatively new and a nobody in the coaching space, but I'm coming up pretty quickly because I'm spending a huge budget marketing myself. We spend anywhere from $60,000 to $144,000 a month on Facebook ads. I'm hiring people like crazy to help me get there quicker. My goal is to get there quicker, spend the money now, so that later I can make more of an impact. And in a couple of years, my profit margin will be better because right now, I'm trying to make my mark.

However quickly you choose to grow, to do exponentially more business, you need support. The key is to figure out your own "highest and best use." In other words, sure, you can do it all (and burn yourself out). But the questions you should be asking are: "What am I doing that no one else can do as well? What am I doing that someone with much less knowledge and training can do? What am I doing that is not my strength and not fun for me?" Those are the things you want someone else to handle.

---

1   http://www.sbmarketingtools.com/much-spend-marketing/

Financial advisor Carol Van Bruggen has never enjoyed research. "In the financial world, you need to do a lot of research. I've never been that good with it and I don't like it. So, I've always made sure that I have people working for me who love it and are great at it."

Attorney Carol Delzer gets support for her social media activities. "The SEO, analytics, getting things posted in the right places, I know it's all important. However, at the end of the day, that's not where I want to put my energy. I could learn it but it's not my expertise. It's not the best use of my time. So, I've hired a part-time person to handle all of that for me."

If you're ready to find the help you need to grow, you'll find lots of leads for virtual assistants via the web. You can find sharp local college students who want to work part-time or semi-retired folks who are eager to keep active. Be very specific about the skills you need and choose someone who is tech-savvy.

When you interview them, just make sure they have the same drive for excellence that you have. Look for someone who is an independent worker. Otherwise, you'll spend too much of your precious time and energy supervising them and correcting their mistakes. Once you hire someone, be *very* clear about what you need them to do. Present a *detailed* job description of what you expect from them before you hire them. And, I know this is hard, but don't hesitate too long before replacing someone who just isn't working out.

So, think about how best to get yourself support. And don't forget that you especially need support in marketing if you want to grow.

If I could only give you three pieces of advice, here's what they would be: 1) **Do video**, no matter what kind of video it is (though an educational piece is best). 2) **Hire an assistant** and make sure it's someone with the same level of ambition you have, and the same desire for excellence and great client service. Even if you need to take out a loan or eat Top Ramen for a month or hire someone on the outside, hire an assistant. This will enable you to do things that you can't do on your own. You'll be able to research the latest technologies or take a class on innovative marketing strategies, then have your assistant implement what you've learned. The more new and innovative techniques and practices you implement, the more you'll reap the benefits in new clients and closings. People do take notice. 3) **Hire a coach**. This is your business and if you want to succeed and truly turn your business into a steam engine that never stops, hire someone to help guide and push you through it. My work stands out. I'm so incredibly busy because I'm running two businesses and because of the value that I give—and I couldn't give all that value without the support of good coaches. (I'll talk more about this in Chapter Eleven.)

Fit Your Business to Your Life

I'd like you to start with the attitude that *you* run your business, *it* doesn't run you. I know, I know—if you're just starting out, it doesn't feel that way. It feels like you have to answer every call at 10pm on Sunday night, chase every slim chance of a potential client, and maybe go to a gazillion networking events. But even if you're a raw newbie, take a deep breath and say, "I run my business. It doesn't run me." And if you've been in your business for 16 years, stop right now and affirm, "From this point on, I run my business. It doesn't run me."

> *"I run my business. It doesn't run me."*

Honestly, people respect you when you have boundaries. They respect you when you tell them that after 7pm you turn your phone off, and that Sundays are family days. Let's be honest, if clients don't respect your boundaries or appreciate that you'll be able to give them better service if you have a little personal time with yourself and your family, then you don't want to work with them anyway.

As a Community Market Leader™, you're not just about making a living. You're creating the life you really want.

Be Intentional with Your Schedule

As service businesses and professionals, many of us get to determine our own working hours. Over the years, I've come to realize that it's not just how many hours you put into your business, it's what you do with those hours (this is a bit different in the service industry i.e. restaurants.)

Early on in real estate, I realized that most agents wander through their days. They stumble out of bed (after hitting the snooze button a few times), shower, grab a cup of coffee and get the kids off. Then they drive to the office, chat with the receptionist, answer a few emails, maybe wander through Facebook, and get another cup of coffee. Then they sit at their desk and say, "Okay, so now what do I need to do today?" Next, they'll settle down to get some work done, get interrupted by phone calls, chat with the guy in the next cubicle who wants to talk about his fishing trip, and stop to go out for lunch. Then they come back, try to get back into what they were doing, look up and suddenly it's 5:00. Time to head home!

This is not the schedule of a Community Market Leader™! Do not fall into this trap!

One of the things I teach all my clients is to get up in the morning (no snooze button!) and start your day by getting your exercise in, getting ready, then doing your morning ritual. Doing your morning ritual is so, so important. The truth is that it's easy to be successful and make money, even though most people don't think that it is. It's the mindset that needs to be shifted. I'm finding with coaching that if I can help my clients break through their mindset, then they have the motivation and energy to do what it takes and follow the strategies I've taught them.

I have every student start their morning ritual in the same way. They get up and they visualize, reading their manifesto. (You'll find an example and a guideline for a manifesto at http://www.theultimatemarketingplaybook.com/member.) They visualize their day, then they write down six things they're grateful for on a Daily Sheet. (Go to http://www.theultimatemarketingplaybook.com/member to download Daily Sheet.) When you show gratitude, you get more of what you're grateful for. Energy goes where focus flows. So, you want to really be grateful for the things you already have.

Next, we have them write out six things that they're going to accomplish and time block them, putting the hardest task first to get it over with. I highly suggest trying to get this done the night before. You'll sleep better and get off to a better start in the morning. By time blocking, I mean that during the time you block out for that project, that's *all* you do. No phone calls, no emails, no interruptions unless the building catches fire! Most of us find that it's best to actually block the same time every day for calls and emails. It's helpful because others begin to expect that they'll hear back from you at a certain time, so they don't bug you. There's a great technique I use called the Pomodoro Technique. With the Pomodoro Technique, by sticking to one task at a time, you can save up to 16 hours a week. (Find out more about this technique at http://www.theultimatemarketingplaybook.com/member.) I don't know about you, but I'd bet saving sixteen hours a week is needed by everyone.

Just by doing these simple things, it helps you learn to be more successful and productive. Showing gratitude, visualizing your day and time blocking all help you keep momentum going and break through any bad stuff that's going on. It's important to do it every single day. It's a huge, huge part of success.

The practice at the end of the day that we teach is equally important. At the end of the day, we have our students celebrate their wins by writing six things they did well throughout the day. Success breeds success. Some people are so focused on all the bad things that happen rather than focusing on the good things. Because that's where their focus is, they end up getting more of the bad things. We want you to focus on all the good things that are working.

> *At the end of the day, we have our students celebrate their wins by writing six things they did well throughout the day. Success breeds success.*

At the end of the day, we have students calendar out their day for the next day. When you calendar out your day for the next day, your mind is already getting shifted as to what that day is going to look like. You then give yourself permission to dream what you need to dream, to let your subconscious work on the issues or problems you need to resolve and work out.

This is how I've put together my own "intentional schedule." I wake up every morning at 5:00. I haven't always done that. I like to sleep. I love to sleep! But I've realized I get so much more energy when I wake up early. I tackle half my day before half the world is even awake. I get up in the morning, do my visualization and gratitude list then go to the gym for an hour five days a week. Next, I come home and hit my emails. I make sure I answer questions and communicate with my clients and students early in the day, so they realize they're important to me.

After emails, I take some kind of educational course for an hour or so. When I take educational courses or online training, it just gives me energy. I'm learning something new and I'm excited about it. I feel alive and awake. With this routine, my day starts with energy, excitement, and enthusiasm.

Next, I look at my monthly and weekly goals and time block the tasks I absolutely need to accomplish that day in order to meet those goals. (We'll talk more about goals in Chapter Ten). When I plan my week, I try to group similar tasks together for efficiency. For example, I might do a bunch of videos on a day when I know I'll be working from home and working on my books or doing coaching calls. I'll try to group outside appointments together on certain days and staff meetings or work at the office on others. I try to make my calls and return calls at the same time each day so I can focus on other work the rest of the day. Just because the phone rings, doesn't mean you have to interrupt what you're doing to answer it!

Do things come up that throw my plans off? Of course! But please notice that I don't start my day by wondering what I could do that day or wandering around on Facebook for inspiration. My friends and family know that when I'm working, I'm working. If it can't wait, I'm there for them. If it can wait, then let it.

One pitfall many professionals fall into is ditching their intentional schedule for a while after a big success. You've landed a plum assignment or contract, and you think, "Woo hoo! Time to party!" Tiffany Rose noticed this trap as a loan officer. "The worst mistake you can do is get a big paycheck and then cool your heels. You have to keep going with your daily routines and your habits and your time blocking. And even if you tell yourself I only want to work four hours today then you better time block and make sure that you set your timer."

Boundaries!

In the beginning when I did everything myself, I had a similar routine to start my day, but it wasn't to this extent. I was at the beck and call of clients and had to put in more hours at the office to get the results I wanted to get. But as you start to grow financially and you get the support you need, you can tweak your business model and how you manage your time.

Now, I tell my clients and students I'm not available on Sundays and I'm not available after 7pm. I tell them I am available 7am to 7pm, Monday through Friday. If it's an emergency, they can call me on Saturday. If Realtors® call me on Saturday, I take their calls or, now more often, I have someone in my office answer it. But I don't take any calls on Sunday. I'll respond to them the next business day.

I learned I had to set clear boundaries with my students, my buyers and their agents, and they respect it. The ones that don't, I don't want to work with. I need downtime so I can stay sharp. You don't owe anyone an explanation. Run your business so you have the personal and family time you need. If you don't, you will burn out and be less effective for your clients. I explain this and my clients almost always understand.

My boundaries help me sustain my energy level. I tell clients and students, "If I worked 24/7, I would not be giving you my best." Everyone needs a day off. Unfortunately, many people just don't recognize this.

What are your boundaries? How do you need to set up your work schedule so you have a healthy balance?
One of my previous business coaches is younger than I am. She teaches professionals how to be better at their jobs. She completely

sets boundaries. When my children were younger and I made client calls from home, I used to worry about it. "If anybody hears my kids in the background, they're going to think I'm unprofessional." But this coach encourages boundaries. During training calls with her, you can hear her kids in the background, yet she's totally focused on you. She gives her family good family time, and her clients good client time. When she works from home, she's so excellent at what she does that I don't think twice about her kids being in the background. I think, "Wow, she's amazing. She's on this call, in her house, with her children, and makes a difference in her kids' lives while making a difference in ours." That's how powerful and good she is at her job. I respect how she has decided to run her business and how she has set her boundaries, because she is giving me incredible value.

On the other hand, if you work from home and treat your business like a hobby instead of a business, it's not going to fly.

Get Better by Keeping Score

As I said, the challenge I've found with many of my students is that I could teach them how to do the strategies, but until they had their mindset right, they weren't successful. Throughout the training and as they're learning what to do, we had to have them keep going back to the mindset part of it. Life happens and it's easy to get discouraged. We remind them to go back to what I call "The Mashore Ramp Up." The ramp up is all about mind set. It's about overcoming limiting beliefs, your belief system about money, creating a new story, having positive affirmations, and learning new strategies to attain clients. You can learn more about "The Mashore Ramp Up," by going to TheUltimateMarketingPlaybook.com/member.

We also do something we call "Setting up Your Work Week for Success." We tell all our students to track their numbers. Not just number of clients coming in but track your efforts on the sales cycle. Track how big your reach was on Facebook, meaning how big the audience was that you're getting. We have students track how many video views they had and how many minutes were viewed. It's basically been proven that when you track numbers, your brain is being coached. That's why athletes track everything. The brain is being coached and then it wants to continue to do better. So, track everything to learn from both your successes and their mistakes.

> *It's basically been proven that when you track numbers, your brain is being coached.*

We've also got our challenge called "3 Clients in 30 Days." (You'll find it at http://www.theultimatemarketingplaybook.com/member). It's actually a 15-day challenge, and we've had students get two, three, six clients in that 15 days. Most of what I'm teaching them is about mindset—and that's where their success comes from. We also teach some of the digital marketing strategies that you're reading about in this book. I'd highly encourage you to join it. It is only $100.00 and you'll receive 15 days of training, and 5 days of pre-training from me while other like-minded businesses and professionals participate with you. We have had over 3,300 people go through this challenge and on average participants pick up 2 new clients, and brick and mortar businesses pick up tons of customers.

Don't Sell Your Soul

Working for yourself can be tough. Most real estate agents need to sell a client's house more than the client does. Most loan officers need to close a loan more desperately than their borrowers. Most insurance brokers need that policy even more than their client does. It comes across in the way they do their business. They're so worried about closing the deal or landing the contract, they forget about the people involved. The work becomes a money thing, not a people thing. Here's where one of my slogans applies again: "People before things, always. If you do your best to take care of people, the things will always come."

> *"People before things, always. If you do your best to take care of people, the things will always come."*

I don't think most people engage in fraudulent behavior—although there are some in any industry. I think many professionals are tempted to do less than their best, to do "what they can get away with." For example, it's not too uncommon to see a loan officer quote rates and terms that are unrealistic. Why? The loan officer probably knows that it won't really happen but, to land the loan, they offered glowing terms to impress the Buyer. Or, it may be tempting to buy lower quality foods to save a buck or two, or be understaffed to save on payroll (nothing bugs me more than going to a restaurant where you want to be served, and having to wait a long time just to get a refill. Seriously, you'll make so much more money giving exceptional service, than that $12.00 an hour you're paying the server). But nothing is worse for a customer or consumer to eat crappy food or have to wait an extra 15 minutes to get a drink because your establishment is understaffed. I personally have left restaurants where I have to wait 15 minutes before someone will offer me a glass of water. I mean let's be real, I could have downed a glass of wine in that 15 minutes (my hubby too), and that one drink alone would have covered the cost of that employee. Start thinking "customer-centric."

Loan officer Debbi Galvan tells a story of borrowers who, even though they liked and trusted her, went to a bank who pulled up their credit report and said they could get them a loan payment that was $200 less than Debbi honestly could. They chose to go with the bank that told them what they wanted to hear. But when they signed, their payment was actually $200 *higher* because the lender had not properly calculated what the taxes were going to be. It was down to the wire and they either signed then or lost the home. The person at the bank simply said, "Oh well that's not my job. That's the escrow company's job." So, they ended up with a loan that was actually worse than what Debbi (who had calculated the taxes correctly) could have done for them. Today, they still refer friends to Debbi, knowing she is honest and trustworthy. By the way, Debbi invested in my coaching program and went from doing only 6 transactions from January to April, and after joining my coaching program, she closed 68 loans in the following 8 months. I know she's going to be reading this and I want to give her a huge shout out and let her know how proud I am of her trusting in herself and taking the leap of faith.

Glenn Hoffman talks about an iffy practice in the insurance industry called "holding the rate." "Insurance rates are cyclical. The go up and they go down. When they go up, of course you have to tell your client the bad news that they need to pay more. But when they go down, some brokers will tell the insurer to 'hold the rate' and revise the policy so that the client still pays that same rate rather than giving the savings to the client. Why do they do this? Because they don't want to explain to their client why the rate dropped, plus the broker's commission is based on that premium. Even though this practice isn't illegal, I believe when a client is eligible for a reduction because they've done a good job or the rates go down, they should get it."

To me and all of the business owners and professionals we interviewed for this book, impeccable integrity is critical to success. Glenn knew one broker who thought that a particular procedure was covered under his client's policy. It turned out that it was not covered. It was the broker's mistake. "He told his client to send the bill to his office and he wrote a check for it himself. That's a guy that stands behind his work. I always want to be that kind of person."

It's all about being on their team, and truly having their best interest at heart. When you sit down with a client who is fixated on unrealistic expectations, you've got your work cut out for you. You need to show up armed with information. And, you need to be willing to walk away.

I didn't get this when I was first entered real estate, but now I am not afraid to say, "Hey, as much as I want your business and know I'm the best person for this job, I'm not going to take your listing. I don't want to waste your time or mine, and I don't want to disappoint you. I know if I take your listing, I will disappoint you. I want to under-promise and over-deliver." In my coaching business, we won't take clients who we feel will not put in the work, or who think that they are going to be successful overnight just by investing. We know that they've got to not only make an investment of money, but an investment of time and resources.

Will you lose that business? Maybe. But usually you gain respect. In another story, Tiffany Rose tells a story about her mom's boss who wanted a certain type of 1% loan on a house that Tiffany knew wasn't the best solution for her. The woman was upset with Tiffany and didn't understand why Tiffany didn't want her to do it. So, the woman walked over to the bank down the street and got the loan she wanted. And about one year later, the bank foreclosed on that woman's new home. Tiffany felt bad for the woman but at least she could feel good about herself that she had tried to steer her in the right direction.

A friend of mine told me a story from when she was in her twenties. She had inherited a bunch of money and decided she wanted to buy a fixer-upper, renovate it, and then sell it. She was pretty naïve back then, but fortunately got hooked up with a very honest real estate agent (who happened to be a single mom and fairly new to the business). My friend found a fixer that she thought was perfect. She was all set to make an offer when her agent said, "I couldn't sleep at all last night thinking about your buying this house. It would be a disaster for you." She pointed out all the problems with the house and how difficult they would be to fix. My friend took her advice and didn't make that offer.

But you know what happened? She bought another fixer through the same agent that was less of a challenge. As my friend became more experienced, she sold the first house and bought another. Then she sold that house and bought a duplex. She ended up buying and selling seven properties in just a few years through her agent. Because the agent had talked her out of that first house, my friend trusted her and became totally loyal.

Trust in any business and profession is about being absolutely trustworthy. It's not about trying to gain someone's trust by looking them sincerely in the eye. It's doing what you need to do to serve your clients' best interests. Even if they don't agree with you. It's your fiduciary duty to educate and inform. Obviously, they hold the cards and can make whatever decisions they want, but it's your job to inform them. Especially when you think they may be in harms way.

You also need to trust your gut and walk away when you need to. I can tell you that we have clients that have come into the coaching program who are totally negative. It always turns out that they're the ones who take up all your time and energy. You just give them all you have and, no matter what, it's never enough. I could actually step in and do all the work for them and they *still* would not succeed because they are so skeptical. Rather than starting with, "I believe in this program and I believe this will work for me," they start out with, "It's not going to work." Then they set out to prove that it doesn't work! Talk about cutting off your nose to spite your face! I believe that you have to be open to, not just the possibility that something might work for you, but the probability that it's going to. When you go into things with that attitude, even if it doesn't turn out exactly as you'd planned, it turns out to your benefit.

When you have a disbelieving attitude, you make all the worst happen for yourself. For example, a woman who joined my program was thinking about going through a divorce and she was super, super negative. We had our mentor coaches helping her and I would help her all the time. No matter what we did for her, after a couple months, she said, "I'm not sure I even want to be in my industry anymore." Then she took off on vacation for a month and came back saying, "It's not working." I said, "Well, you were just on vacation for a month and you haven't been doing anything." But she argued, complaining that the program didn't work and that it sucked. Then she told me, "I'm going to tell everyone this program doesn't work, Krista. And if they join it and ask, I'm going to tell them it doesn't work." I said, "Look, it works great for others. It doesn't work for you because you're not working it."

Finally, I decided that she was so negative that I didn't want her in the program. She was wasting everyone's time. So, even though she'd been in the program for five months and we could prove she didn't do 80% of what she was supposed to, we gave her all her money back. She had every excuse in the world, from sick kids to vacations. Then of all things, when I tried to give her money back, she said, "Oh my god. I'm going to sue you if you do that. I have a contract and blah blah blah." I said, "Look, you're saying you don't want this. You're saying you're unhappy. Now I'm giving you your money back and you're telling me you're going to sue me because I'm giving you your money back?!?" Honestly, she was a Negative Nellie. I'm guessing nothing in her life worked for her, at least in her eyes. If I'd given her Aladdin's lamp and all she had to do was rub it, she would have complained it was ugly and thrown it out!

So, don't let yourself get roped into impossible clients. Glenn Hoffman will "fire" clients who are abusive to his staff. Writer Heather Estay broke off with a client who insisted on using ethnic and racial slurs in his book. She also won't work for someone who tries to take credit for other people's work. "In a way, there's nothing new under the sun and all ideas come from somewhere. But this woman was trying to claim credit for a specific process another person developed—and I knew this because that other person happened to be a former client of mine!" You don't have to be desperate and work with clients that give you ulcers. Go for those clients that make you feel good about the work you do.

And don't be tempted to fudge a little bit, even if you see others do it in your industry. It is *not* necessary for your success. In fact, it comes back later to bite those who engage in it. You simply don't need to work the system. As a Community Market Leader™, doing all the things a Community Market Leader™ does, you'll have plenty of clients and make all the money you want. And you'll sleep well at night.

To Learn More about Becoming a Community Market Leader, visit

KristaMashore.com

CHAPTER TEN

READY, SET, GOALS!

If you're a person who aims high in life and I've done my job in writing this book, you're probably eager to get started on the path to become a Community Market Leader™ and reap all the benefits that go with it. Good for you! You've spent time in the prior chapters thinking about your "*why*." Now let's put together a plan to get you where you want to go. To start, it's important to understand how to set effective goals so when the going gets a little tough—which it will—you have the juice to keep going to achieve what you're after. It takes work to get what you want, but you can do anything you put your mind to.

I've always been the kind of person who decides what she wants and goes for it. I was setting goals long before I really knew how to do it. My goals—and my determination to achieve them—have helped me create an incredible business and a really satisfying personal life. I'd like the same for you. I've studied a lot of different goal-setting systems and taken what I think is the best from each. If your goals have produced mediocre results so far, it might be due to the specific *way* you're setting goals.

Your Vision is your Magic Genie

Now here's the deal. If you're like me (in the past) I'd read this type of thing and think, "Oh, I've got this, I don't need goal setting, I know what I want." But please, let me forewarn you. There is a reason that all the great self-help books in the world always talk about goal setting. So, listen up, be open minded and let's get into the "how" that makes the "what" happen.

In working with goals, you have to begin with the big picture before you narrow it down into smaller goals and tasks. This is on the level of "What inspires me?" It's very similar to your "why," but it's fleshed out in technicolor. It's that clear vision of what you ultimately want.

> *In working with goals, you have to begin with the big picture before you narrow it down into smaller goals and tasks.*

For example, I mentioned that one of my "why's" is to spend more quality time with my family. Here's what that looks like in vision form:

> *We have a blended family, but by looking at us you would never know it. My relationship with my stepson is stronger than ever, and he confides in me because he trusts me to keep what he says confidential. My daughters have so much confidence that when they walk into the room you can't help but notice. For all of us, our main mission in life is to be good and to help others succeed and become better. Our family makes it a priority to spend time together and we put each other first. Our entire family is full of abundance and gratitude and we take nothing for granted. All of this stems from the fact that my husband and I are so strongly connected.*

When I stop and visualize this, I get excited and happy. I can practically taste how sweet this is! It's not yet set up in "end goal" form (which I'll show you next), but it is definitely inspirational.

In his book, *Awaken the Giant Within: How to Take Immediate Control of Your Mental, Emotional, Physical, and Financial Destiny*, Tony Robbins outlines how he starts the process of setting goals. I like this process because you can do it in less than an hour and don't have to spend hours and hours sweating over goal setting.

You begin by brainstorming, writing down possibilities very quickly so you don't censor yourself. In this first stage, don't get hung up on the details of *how* to make this happen, but let it flow and fill in details later. You need to make this first list fun and inspirational. Remember how you felt when you were a kid about the things you wanted to be or have? Your list of goals should make you feel excited like that.

Tony divides goals up into four categories: Personal Development, Career and Financial, Toys and Adventure, and Contribution goals. Personally, I prefer the categories of Marriage, Family, Business, Personal, and Giving Back. Divide your goals into any categories that make sense to you.

Within each of your categories, brainstorm a list of goals for five minutes. My list under Family looks something like this:

- *Kids all being close and getting along*
- *More connection with my stepson*
- *My daughters feel more self-confident*
- *Our family focuses on giving*
- *Spending quality time together*
- *Working together in my business*
- *Strong connection with my husband, putting him first always*

When your list is complete, take one minute to give each goal a timeframe of 1 year, 2 years, or 3 years, and mark them as 1 (taking 1 year or less), 2, or 3. (Most of the items on my list above are within one year.) Next, choose one of your 1-year or less goals that is most important and write for two minutes about *why* it's so important to you. Done! Go to the next category and do the same process.

Using part of my vision above, I might write something like: *I have more connection with my stepson so he will confide in me because I know it's tough to be a young man and I know I can help him. I contribute to his life. I love him and I know he feels that love. I know he feels the certainty that, no matter what happens, I've got his back.*

What is your vision in each of your categories? I highly recommend you stop and do this 30-minute process and create your vision in at least one category before I show you how to create specific end goals.

Here's another personal example, my vision in the Business category:

> *My Community Market Leader® coaching and training is very successful and growing exponentially. My Homes by Krista business is also thriving and both businesses are running like well-oiled machines. My husband and three children all work alongside me. Our mission is to encourage others and help them live more prosperous lives. Both businesses are recognized nationally within our industry. I totally enjoy speaking to large groups and am thrilled that I am making such a difference in the lives of others.*

That may not be your personal vision, but can't you see how a vision like that would get you leaping out of bed in the morning, eager to dive into your day? That's what you want for your own vision. Take a few minutes and go through the 30-minute process to jot down your vision and why you want it.

End Goals: Stepping Stones to Your Vision

In his training sessions, Dr. Matthew James, CEO of The Empowerment Partnership who has taught Neuro Linguistic Programming (NLP) for about 30 years, emphasizes setting effective goals. He calls your vision "aim goals." An aim goal is the direction you want to go in life. It never really has an end point, but it inspires you to keep moving forward. Dr. James says that an "end goal" is different. It's a specific result you want and after you achieve it, you move on to another end goal. Your end goals are like stepping stones

> *Your end goals are like stepping stones toward your vision.*

157

toward your vision. To set end goals, Dr. James uses the acronym "SMART" (like many other teachers). Where an aim goal (vision) can be broad, your end goal has to be SMART.

S: The S stands for *specific* and *simple*. If your end goal isn't specific, you don't have a clear target. For example, if you say, "I want to make lots of money," what does that even mean? Thirty thousand per year? Four million per year? When you put a specific number to it, you can picture that result and begin to figure out what to do to get there. So, you might write down, "I am making $10,000 a month by June 30, 20XX without having to work weekends and late nights."

Simple means that it is basic enough to explain to a 7-year-old. In his trainings, Dr. James explains that your unconscious mind (which is always at work to support you) needs very simple instructions. So, it's better to say, "I have a steady net income of $27,000 per month" rather than, "I want my portfolio to earn an average of 3.7% while I close 5 loans per month, so my commissions total $22,500 and I pick up an additional $3,500 in referral fees." Too complicated! Keep it simple.

M: The M stands for *measurable* and *meaningful*. If you can't measure your end goal, how will you know when you've gotten there? Some goals are easier to measure than others. Take the example of my family goals: How will I know when my stepson and I are closer? I might set the end goal to be, "My stepson and I talk for five to ten minutes at least twice per week, and we go out to lunch alone at least once per month." That's something I can measure.

Meaningful means that the end goal has to be important to *you*. Sometimes we try to create goals based on what other people want for us or what we think we *should* do. Those goals won't inspire us. If your goal is to work with sixteen different clients this month or this quarter because your brother thinks you should, how exciting is that? But, if *you* decide you want to work with sixteen because you're determined to expand your practice, or because you want to pay off your debts so you can sleep at night, that goal will have some real juice behind it.

A: According to Dr. James, A stand for three things: *achievable, all areas of your life,* and *as if now. Achievable* means that on some level you believe you can achieve this goal. That's not to say that the goal should be easy. Easy goals aren't very exciting. Your goal should be a stretch and take some extra effort and focus on your part. But, if in your heart, you're convinced you can't hit your goal, you'll be fighting yourself the whole way. Take your "impossible" goal and just back off a notch. If you think designing ten houses this month is impossible for you, set your goal at seven. Then, when you hit that goal, set your next goal up to eight or nine.

All areas of your life means to take into consideration your life balance. For example, if you're setting a huge goal for your business this year, where will that additional time and energy come from? How can you make sure that you don't mess up your personal life, your health, and your sanity while pursuing your big goal? If you simply put blinders on and focus solely on one goal, you'll find that other areas will suffer—and when they do, you'll get thrown off course. You may have to get creative and figure out ways to keep all areas of your life on track as you pursue your big goals.

As if now means that goals are always stated in the present. Rather than saying, "I *will* make $4M in 20XX," you keep it in present tense and say, "I *make* $4M in 20XX." There are a number of reasons for this. First, it keeps you accountable. When you say that you *will* do something, it is always out somewhere in the future. When someone else points out, "Hey, but you're *not* doing that," you always have the excuse of, "Yeah, but I *will* someday." When you state, "I *am* doing this," you can look yourself in the mirror and know if it's true or not.

R: The R stands for *realistic* and *responsible.* Even though your goal is possible based on everything in your life right now, is it realistic? A lot of seemingly impossible things really are possible. The question is whether it's realistic to expect that end result for you at this time. Maybe you need more training, or to build a stronger foundation to reach your end goal. If so, those things should be set as your first goals.

Responsible has to do with what NLP calls "ecology." Is your goal good not only for you but also for the other people involved—your family, your community, and even our planet? If your goal does harm in any way, you'll run into a lot of resistance, not only from the outside but from within yourself as well.

T: The T is for *timed* and *toward what you want*. Your end goal has to have a specific timeframe so you'll know how much energy it will take to achieve it. For example, say you want to double your business. The goal, "I double the revenue from my business within three months from now" is a totally different animal than "I double the revenue from my business within the next three years." Use a specific date for your goal and calendar it so you can keep track of your progress.

Toward what you want means to set a positive goal, not a negative one. Negative goals are, "I am no longer 40 pounds overweight" or "I do not have to scramble every month to pay my bills." Research shows that when people have negative goals, they lose motivation as they get closer to the end result. So, when that person hits the point where he is only *ten* pounds overweight or where she can cover *most* of her bills, they stop feeling as stressed so they slack off. With a positive goal, you're inspired to keep going until you feel the reward of the achievement. To turn them into positive goals, those negative goals could be rewritten as, "I weigh 180 pounds" or "I have an extra $1,000 in my account after paying off all my bills each month."

Personally, when I'm learning something new, I find examples very helpful. Here are some examples of well-written, SMART end goals and others that are not.

GOOD: My CML® business nets over $6M by March 21, 20XX

NOT GOOD: My CML® business will take off and be highly successful sometime next spring.

GOOD: By May 15, 20XX, I have booked four 3-day CML® trainings and signed up 4,500 participants.

NOT GOOD: Next year, I will do several trainings in front of huge audiences for my CML® business.

GOOD: As of December 15, 20XX, I am working 1 hour per day at Homes by Krista and 7 hours per day at CML® coaching and training.

NOT GOOD: Before next year, I will work less on Homes by Krista and more on my coaching and training, while still getting more personal time.

GOOD: As of January 1st, 20XX, my husband and I dedicate one evening per week to each other, going out and doing something fun together. (We actually do this every week. I highly recommend you do too. If your partnership is strong, you'll show up better in the world!)

NOT GOOD: By next year, my husband and I will be spending more quality time together.

Putting it All Together

Begin with your visions (or aim goals) then translate them into good end goals. I've come to understand end goals should be three-month goals or shorter. Anything farther down the road than that is less effective. Why? We're now an instant gratification culture. Brian P. Morgan who co-authored the book, *The 12 Week Year: Get More Done in 12 Weeks than Others Do in 12 Months,* said that people who set goals in three month increments get more done toward their goals in that timeframe than most people do in a whole year. It also allows us to get smaller wins along the way and that sense of success breeds more success.

> *end goals should be three-month goals or shorter. Anything farther down the road than that is less effective.*

Write your goals down. Even if you have no idea how to achieve a goal, write it down and think about it every day. Place your vision (longer term) and end goals (three months or less) on your bathroom mirror, put them on your steering wheel, tape them to your laptop screen. Every time you see them, think about *why* you want those goals. Read them every morning when you wake up and every night before you go to sleep. I even read them aloud into my iPhone so I can listen to them as often as I can whenever I have a minute. Be sure to look at your short term (12 week) goals every week so you can see your progress and know what you need to do to guarantee you'll achieve them.

I also like to create vision boards. I use a poster board and find pictures that represent what I'm going after. I might have a family on a beach for a vacation I want, or a graph showing a business increasing its profits. Whenever I look at my vision boards, I remind myself of why I want those things and how great it will feel when I get there.

A friend of mine even used a vision board to lose weight. She had been on some medication that caused her to gain 30 pounds in a very short time. It freaked her out to see herself in the mirror. She gathered photos of herself at her normal weight and lots of pictures of slim bodies. She plastered them all over her mirror so that when she looked in the mirror, that's all she saw—not her overweight self. She says this vision "board" inspired her to do all the things she needed to do to become her prior size again.

Next, take action on your end goals. Every day take one step, big or small, that moves you closer to that goal. Having a dream without clearly written goals is just a fantasy. And **a goal without action behind it is just fiction.**

> *Having a dream without clearly written goals is just a fantasy. And **a goal without action behind it is just fiction.***

Activities toward your goals should show up on your calendar. If they don't, your goal must not be very important to you, right?

The action steps you take toward your goals don't have to be huge, but they do need to be consistent. For example, you may have a goal to "Create a digital marketing platform by December 1, 20XX." You might start by researching various Landing Page Software, then setting a deadline to choose one. You might set a date to create your own first three videos or learn how to run ads on your favorite social media site. The important thing is to do something that takes you one step closer to your goal every day.

Your Community Market Leader™ Start-Up Plan

Now that you have the process for setting goals, let's create a series of goals around becoming a Community Market Leader™. This is important. Take the time to do it and please reach out to me once you do and tell me about your successes. I'm excited to see and hear about your growth. Please email me your successes to Krista@KristaMashore.com or #CommunityMarketLeader.

First, write down your vision of what that will look like when you've achieved it. How do you feel? What in your life looks different professionally, personally, and within your family? What kind of business will you have? Who will be working with you? How will your days be spent? What kind of income will you bring in?

Next, spend a few minutes to write down *why* you want this. How does it make your life better? What would be exciting about it to you?

Now set up a number of end goals (three months or less) using the SMART acronym. I'd suggest you put them in these categories (you'll notice that some overlap):

Engaging the Community

Creating Educational Videos

Creating an Online Presence

Engaging Past Customers or Clients

Self-Education

Researching Trends in the My Business, My Profession and My Market

Updating and Employing Technology

Personal Growth

Enhancing My Professional Skills

Learning Best Practices in Business and My Profession

Setting Up My CRM

Offers and Giveaways to Bring in Customers and Clients

Creating My Plan for My Complete Sales Cycle: My Funnel

Using Social Media for Marketing and Community Engagement

Revamping My Current Marketing Materials

Identifying My Client Avatar

Developing My Brand and Niche

Solidifying Your Business

Identifying Resources

Hiring Assistant (s) or Employee (s) for Key Areas

Creating a Team

Systematizing All Processes, Start to Finish

Okay, deep breath! I know it may sound overwhelming but it's all doable. Just take it a step at a time.

Within each of these categories, figure out what tasks you want to get accomplished in 30 days, 60 days, and 90 days to get you started in that area. For example, in Revamp My Current Marketing Materials, maybe your tasks are 1. Pull them all out to see what we've got, 2. Decide which are useful and which should be tossed, 3. Hire a graphic designer. You don't have to complete the entire category. Write those tasks down as SMART end goals. What can you do alone and where do you need assistance? To get you started, here are some Action Challenges that will yield fast results, and that you can *easily* accomplish within the first 90 days:

Action Challenge #1: Create your first educational video: Choose a relevant topic that is getting a lot of buzz right now and create a 30-second video about it. Go to your business, professional publications or Google to find a good topic. Do not get stumped and don't over think it—just do it! Use your iPhone to record the video. When it's done, just publish it. If you want a higher quality video just send it to Fiverr or another source to have it edited and annotations added. Then upload it on social media sites like Facebook, Instagram, and Twitter. Done! Honestly, you don't even need to get it edited. I just want you taking action. This seems scary at first, but it gets easier and easier as time goes by. Staying consistent and just doing it is key.

> *This seems scary at first, but it gets easier and easier as time goes by. Staying consistent and just doing it is key.*

Action Challenge #2: Gather client testimonials: Contact past clients to get testimonials to post online. Create an email and send it out, including links to Yelp, Google, and any sites relevant to your business or profession. Send your first email out to at least forty clients using some kind of incentive (see example email below). Then send a similar email out to five other past clients every week. (It doesn't look good to get a ton of reviews one week then nothing for months, so stay consistent in this.) Put it on the calendar so you remember to do this consistently, rather than getting a bunch of testimonials all in one shot. Also, put it on your fulfillment check list to ask for testimonials after ending your work with your client.

Here's an example email I've used in my real estate business that got some great testimonials:

Subject Line: Thank you so much for Everything!! I'd love to enter you into a drawing for $250.00 and I'm only sending this to a total of 40 people, so the chances of winning are high.

Dear [Name of Homeowner],

I hope all is well with you :-)

I was hoping that you could help me. I'm very much trying to enhance my on-line presence. The best way is actually through Zillow and Google+. YELP is also huge! Would you mind taking a few minutes to write a review for me? Zillow attracts about 90,000 viewers each month alone, just in your zip code. So, many people are looking and using these services to help find their agent. It will definitely help me increase my business. I know you are so incredibly busy, so you'll be enrolled in a drawing for a $250.00 Amazon card.

Here are the links to leave the reviews on Zillow, Trulia, Yelp, & Google My Business (include links here)

I appreciate your time and efforts. Thanks so very much.

Your Real Estate Professional for LIFE

Krista Mashore

Obviously, you should write an email that sounds like you, not like me. Even better, create a *video* request for testimonials. Your email can have the same subject line and an individualized greeting, but the video can be made as a generic request. Send a request out to a minimum of five people every week. Before you do this, send a video text message telling them to check their email for a chance to win a drawing of $250.00 (or whatever your incentive is) so they know to look out for it. But remember, the more personalized the video is (stating someones name) the better results you'll get.

If you're a brick and mortar, be sure your employees (I like to call them team mates) ask for testimonials as well.

Action Challenge #3: Generate Leads Online: Create a landing page, I use ClickFunnels. If you'd like to subscribe to ClickFunnels, go to www.kristamashore.com/clickfunnels you can get a free 2 week trial, but don't do this until you're ready so you can utilize your free trial to it's fullest advantage. I love ClickFunnels, and this is where I build all of my Landing Pages and Funnels. If you saw this book online, more than likely, you bought it through one of my book funnels. After setting up a landing page, create some kind of offering (free download of valuable information, a calculator related to your business, or a free phone consultation) that will attract the types of clients you want. Hire Freelancer, Fiverr, or any other resource to get you going on this. Look for eye-catching photos that stand out and tell a story that reflects your avatar's needs and desires.

Be creative! Don't just title your page, "Find Out How Much You Need to Retire." Brainstorm innovative headlines. "Can You Retire Earlier Than You Thought?" or "Will your Retirement Plan Lead You to Retirement Hell or Retirement Heaven?"

Next, create an ad that directs your targeted audience to the landing page you created to attract the people you want. (In our coaching sessions, we teach people exactly how to set up targeted audiences on different social media platforms.) Post the ad on several social media platforms. Spend at least $20 on each ad. On my real estate ads I spend around $200, but I spend more on my coaching ads because they are national. Schedule a new ad to run twice every month. Pay attention to which ads and which platforms get you the most response. We run twenty to thirty ads at any one given time with different and similar offers and we constantly change the copy, colors, pictures etc. and test which offers perform the best (AdEspresso.com can help with this).

Action Challenge #4: Generate More Leads Online: Calculators and free relevant and useful information are great tools to attract people and capture their contact information, but what else can you think of? The key is that it needs to be something that is truly *valuable* to people.

One program that has worked incredibly well for me is called The Local Heroes Program. I teamed up with a local lender and we offer discounts to teachers, fire fighters, police officers, and men and women in the military—basically anyone who serves the community. You could do something similar as a personal trainer, financial planner, or small business consultant. On the program my lender and I developed, we offered special discounts:

1. $100 off a home inspection
2. Reimbursement on appraisals ($500+ dollar value)
3. Reimbursement of termite inspection ($250 value)
4. $1,000 towards closing costs

Our only disclaimer is: "If buyer fails to purchase for any reason, the buyer will incur the costs. Offer only valid for one home."

If you were in the military or on the police force, wouldn't you be attracted to that page?

Your action challenge is to come up with at least five ideas for landing pages that offer value to a certain segment of your market. What special value could you offer? Come up with your ideas and implement one per month by creating a landing page then posting an ad for it on social media (you'll reach far more people if you sponsor or pay for your ad). Not all of your ideas will be home runs. But the ones that are can be gold!

Action Challenge #5: Create Your First Informational Video: Choose a particular issue of your target market and study it. For example, if you're a therapist who works with children, how about "Five Ways Parents Can Help Children Learn in Crowded Classrooms"? Or as a landscape architect, "Three Hottest Trends for Drought Resistant Lawns." Or as an attorney specializing in Trusts, "Four Critical Considerations People Miss in Creating Their Trust."

Again, don't stress over this! Gather your information and think about what that information means to potential clients. Then just be conversational, as if you met someone at a party who asked you about that topic. Once your video is complete, just upload it, or shoot it off to Fiverr for editing and adding annotations. Upload it on social media sites like Facebook, Instagram, and Twitter. Email it to your contact list and ask for feedback.

Action Challenge #6: Create Some "Keeping Connected" Videos: Brainstorm at least ten videos you can send out to various people (clients, past clients, people who give you leads, prospective clients, or anyone in your sphere of influence). For example, your video might say, "Thanks for trusting your mortgage to me" or "I hope your yoga training is giving you good results" or Hey I just saw that little Johnny just hit a home run, nice job." It could be a Happy Birthday or Happy Anniversary video, or a Get Well Soon video. Set aside fifteen minutes *every day* to send out five videos. Work your way up to ten a day, you'll be amazed at the positive results you get. Remember, don't ask for business, just be conversational and recognize something they've done.

This may seem like a lot. But think of it as making five quick phone calls. The videos can be brief and casual. They do *not* have to be perfect—in fact, it's better if they aren't. Do this for at least thirty days straight before you decide whether this practice is worth continuing—I definitely think it is! (Remember that you can make some of these videos generic to send to anyone then simply personalize the subject line. That saves time, but the more a video speaks directly to an individual, the better the results you'll get.)

Action Challenge #7: Update Your Use of Technology: If you want to evolve, become better and better, be unique and stand out, it's imperative that you incorporate new technologies and innovations into your business. This is an on-going process and should not be taken lightly. For this challenge, watch a minimum of one webinar or take one training on an aspect of technology that you know you need to improve in your business. We have great technical trainings on my coaching site. Go to http://www.theultimatemarketingplaybook. com/member for more information. Implement *at least one new strategy* from these trainings within the first ninety days. It might mean doing a target market ad campaign on social media or creating a landing page. Don't try to do everything at once, but master each new technology and strategy then implement the next one. Be consistent about this. If you're standing still in terms of technology, you're actually falling behind.

Action Challenge #8: Upgrade Your Marketing and Promotional Materials: Some of you might be saying, "What marketing and promotional materials?!?" If you really don't have any, this is when you start to develop some. If you have some that are standard in your industry (we have scads of marketing materials in real estate), this is when you revise yours, so they stand out. These materials can be hand-outs, brochures, informational pieces, even your signage and business card. And you want to come up with a system for getting these pieces out of your office and into the world!

For example, you can send postcards with checklists pertinent to your industry that people would find valuable: "What you Need to Save for Tax Time." "Tips to help Your Child Get Excited About School." "How to Lose That Extra Ten Pounds from the Holidays." Like everything you do, get creative and think about topics that would provide real value to recipients.

Think of five topics relevant to your business or profession that you could put on the back of your post cards/marketing materials that would be useful for your particular community. Your focus should be, "What can I do to serve them? What information will be useful to them? What coupons, discounts or special offers, could be valuable to them.?"

Create a brochure about you and what makes you stand out. Why should someone work with you? Mention all of your accolades and credentials, include raving customer reviews. Include all the innovative, tech-savvy processes you have. Include a bit about your personal story and why they should chose you and your business or profession. If you have a great track record, showcase it. If you don't yet, showcase achievements in other areas that represent your value and work ethic.

These eight challenges will help kick-start you on your way to becoming a Community Market Leader™. But you'll need to take consistent action in several areas to really see the benefits. As you set your goals and create your action plan, don't just try something a couple of times and give up on it. Innovation, implementation, and consistency are the keys to growth. I always tell my students, "Learning is great but if you don't take action and implement it's not worth the time to learn."

CHAPTER ELEVEN

DON'T JUST SURVIVE, THRIVE (EVEN IN A BAD ECONOMY)!

In my first book, I wrote, *"The reason I love continually learning is that I know there's a better, more effective way to do almost anything—even if you're already good at that thing. That's why I dive into situations that might stretch my thinking and challenge how I do things. Learning even one small thing each day allows me to keep expanding into the next 'better way.'"* Just as important, I *implement* that better way and continue to improve on it.

> *The reason I love continually learning is that I know there's a better, more effective way to do almost anything— even if you're already good at that thing.*

If you want to become a Community Market Leader™, you'll need to stretch and grow. You'll need to step out of your very comfy comfort zone and do things you've never tried before. And here's the deal: Even after you look around and see that you're now dominating your market or business, your presence is everywhere and clients are flocking to your door, you *still* need to keep growing.

A Community Market Leader™ is more like a verb than a noun. It's not a place you get to where you can sit back, settle in and take a nap. A Community Market Leader™ is a state of mind that has you continually improving, innovating, learning, and expanding in your mastery. And, if you ever get tired of your industry, you can apply that mindset to the next great thing you decide to do.

Growth is scary, but it's also exhilarating. And, more often than not, the thing that is scariest to you is the thing that will propel you to a new level. Controlled growth is the focus. This means growing and expanding after we've mastered the previous growth. You implement one new tool and become an expert in it prior to implementing new growth tools.

One of the scariest things I've ever done in real estate is to create my videos. When you meet me I'm super enthusiastic and outgoing, but that doesn't mean that I love doing videos and public speaking. In fact, I am not a natural public speaker. I actually *am super fearful* of public speaking. I get anxious and have actual panic attacks. In the old days when I did broker tours, I'd stand in front of twenty people I knew, and my palms would sweat, and I'd be so nervous that I could hardly remember what I was supposed to say. One time, I even called myself Krista Miller, and at the time I was Krista Mashore.

The idea of being in front of a camera to make a video that literally thousands of people might see was terrifying to me. Then, I figured out how valuable videos can be. Was I great when I started doing it? Nope. I had no idea what I was doing, and I was so nervous that I spoke even faster than I normally do, kind of like those disclaimers at the end of prescription drug ads on T.V.

But I learned and got better and better. And I felt excited and proud of myself each time I saw myself getting better. It helped me in all areas of my life, and I stopped worrying so much that people were judging me or that I might make a mistake. Even when I wasn't that great at it, I made an impact and stood out from the crowd. When I look back at my old videos, I can honestly say that they were horrible. Now they're much better. One video used to take me an hour. Now I can do one in literally five minutes.

When I wanted to expand into coaching, the whole public speaking thing came up again. The Universe apparently thinks it's funny that we have to face our biggest fears to get what we want! But again, I realized that making presentations and talking to large organizations was important to launching this new business. So, I pulled up my Big Girl panties and did it!

To get to where you want to be, you may have to do things you're afraid of doing. But look at the alternative: Many professionals spend their careers being constantly afraid of where their next client is coming from. They're scared that their business isn't going to sustain itself. They're hamsters running on that wheel, operating basically out of fear about whether they'll be able to make enough money to cover their own bills and whether they'll be able to close the next loan or fill enough classes to cover the rent.

Personally, I'd rather face the fears of growing better and getting stronger, so I never again have those kinds of worries. I know that my pipeline will always be as full as I want it to be. I know that my businesses are sustainable no matter what the economy is doing because I'm always adapting and changing. Right now, video is working magnificently but that doesn't mean it always will. I'm constantly adding and changing what and how I do videos so they continue to stand out.

For example, when I first started, my videos were about three minutes long. Now I've learned that shorter videos, around thirty seconds, are much more effective. I'm still learning and striving to be better. Had I not kept in touch with research and change, I wouldn't know this. I've also learned that highly polished videos at certain stages of the funnel, actually under-perform the videos that are more real and raw. Keep testing, changing and adapting what you are doing so you not only survive but thrive!

Most of us have reasons for not facing our fears. If I don't have a reason to cross over a river full of crocodiles then, heck no! I'm not doing it. But, if one of my daughters were in danger, or the thing I most wanted in the world was on the other side? You bet I'll cross it. In fact, I'd run right through those crocs to save my daughters or a loved one! The most important question you can ask yourself is, "Why do I want this?" Why are you reading this book? Why do you want to expand in your business or profession? What will more consistent and greater income bring you? What would that look like for you personally, spiritually, within your family, and within yourself?

I'm not really fearful anymore but I certainly was when I first left my teaching profession and dove into real estate full time. And I was scared to death when I started my coaching and training business. I had the same fear we all have of, "Oh, my God, how am I going to pull this off?" But I made the decision, "Okay, Krista, you'll just have to stand out and be different, and learn how to be better than everyone else. You need to march in there and *just do it*, because failure is not an option." One of my good friends Alisha Collins from Wyoming says, "We do what other people **won't** do today, so we **can** do what others **can't** later."

Why Do You Want This?

I've talked about this throughout the book and you may be wondering why the heck I'm bringing it up again. Well, it's because if your "why" is clear enough and strong enough, everything, I mean *everything*, will fall into place. And if your why is fuzzy and uninspiring, *everything* will be a grind. And the odds of your giving up before you achieve the life you want will be very high. I don't want that for you.

I didn't have to discover my "why" when I started in real estate because it was staring me in the face. I had to support myself and my two little girls. Giving up or just skating by was not an option for me. Any time it got rough in the business, I just had to think about feeding my girls and making sure they had a roof over their heads. That motivation got me through all kinds of difficult times and inspired me to keep finding ways to better myself and my business.

Starting my coaching business was different. I felt an urgent desire, a passion to help others achieve the kind of success I had achieved and that I knew was possible for them. People thought I was nuts to build a brand-new business when my real estate business was so successful. But I *had* to! And that strong desire has driven me to overcome all kinds of fears and obstacles to build this new business very quickly.

Finding out your "why" is probably the most important key to your success in anything. Why do you want to be a Community Market Leader™? Yes, it will bring you

> *Finding out your "why" is probably the most important key to your success in anything.*

more money/clients/recognition. But why do you want these things? Your "why" is what is going to drive you. Your "why" is the force that keeps you going when you want to quit.

As I'm writing this book, I'm also developing more training materials, training and coaching hundreds of people, running my real estate business and managing my "Teens Lifting Lives" non-profit program. My husband says, "You need to stop and take more time off." I tell him I can't stop. I need to push right now so that eventually *all* I'm doing is my coaching and training. That's my true passion and love. That's my "why."

My "why" is very specific. I am on a path of changing my professional career completely. I'm a very successful Realtor®, and I love it. My new personal "why" is coaching and helping others use digital marketing strategies, and it's what I am passionate about. I love making a positive impact on people. I want to empower people. I love inspiring people. I want to make people, like you, empowered in their business so you can lead the kind of life I'm living right now. I want to help other people enjoy prosperity, have more free time, and really enjoy what they're doing and feel good about it. My overall goal is to create Community Market Leaders™ across the country who are so successful that they become philanthropists in their communities and give back. I want it to be a worldwide movement. I declare this daily in my own personal manifesto which you can also see on the website I've mentioned previous.

My daily affirmations include a bunch of statements that support this: "I positively affect every life I touch." "I am the number one trainer and coach in the world." "I love public speaking." "I speak slowly, and my words are impactful." "I make a difference." "I am a Go-Giver." I have several others, but you get the gist. Sometimes, at first, we need to fake ourselves out until we actually do believe in our dreams. (To hear my daily affirmations, go to http://www.theultimatemarketingplaybook.com/member.)

Why is becoming a Community Market Leader™ important to you? What is going on in your life that you want to be different? What is your passion and how will stepping up your game in your business or profession support that?

One of my favorite teachers, Tony Robbins, says, *"People are not lazy. They simply have impotent goals - that is, goals that do not inspire them."* It's your inspirational "why" that will get you across that crocodile-infested river or get you in front of a video camera. It's your powerful dream, or the thing you love, that will help you face your biggest fears, encourage you to change the "safe" ways you've always done things, and keep you going as you're learning and feeling out of your comfort zone.

> *"People are not lazy. They simply have impotent goals - that is, goals that do not inspire them."*

What is your "why?" Do you want to make more money? And, if you do, *why* do you want to make more money? Do you want more time? More time for what? Do you crave financial freedom? Do you want to pay off your house and become debt free? Do you need to have less anxiety? Write down all of your "why's." Please do me a favor and don't skip this. Your "whys" are what make you do and act on what you need to in order to get the outcome that you want.

Who Do You Need to Be for the Business You Want?

I love this other quote from Tony Robbins:

> *"Beliefs have the power to create, and the power to destroy. Human beings have the awesome ability to take any experience of their lives, and create a meaning that disempowers them, or one that can literally save their lives."*

To become the Community Market Leader™ you want to be, you'll need to get rid of any limiting beliefs or doubts you might have. If you have any limiting beliefs, take them out of your head. If any type of negative thought comes in, change it around, and know that you deserve this, that you can do this, that this is attainable. In my "Teens Lifting Lives" group, one of the girls, Samantha, posted this on Facebook: "As Krista constantly drills into our heads to take the negative beliefs out and put the positive in, the more I do this the easier it becomes."

What I've taught you in this book is absolutely attainable. I doubt anyone else is doing it in your business or profession. You'll be the one to do it before anyone else does, and you're going to be successful at it. I need you to know that you're worthy and deserving of greatness. You deserve this.

Early on, I watched a webinar called Stealth Seminar. It's not real estate related, but I was learning how to do webinars and I wasn't completely comfortable making videos. I was already creating educational videos for my niches, and training buyers and sellers through webinars. But I knew I had a lot to learn. The guy teaching the class was so dorky, so frumpy. My first impression was "I can't believe this guy is on video." But after twenty seconds of watching him, I loved him. He was super smart, he was funny, and he definitely knew what he was talking about. I liked him even more because he was on camera being himself—frumpy and dorky and nerdy.

In fact, in one of his first videos, he was picking his nose and scratching his butt as he was getting ready to do a training and the camera was on him. I don't know if he did that on purpose or not, but it was hysterical. He didn't care that people were watching. He was just very real.

We're all unique in our own way, and you don't want to change to become just like me or just like anyone. As you change and grow, **you want to become more like yourself, not less**. To get the results of a Community Market Leader™, you need to do the things a Community Market Leader™ does—but in your own unique way.

*As you change and grow, **you want to become more like yourself, not less**.*

I was raised in a very religious family, and I rebelled growing up. I was super close to my family, but I ended up getting into trouble, going to juvenile hall, spent a year in a group home and then I landed in a foster home and spent my high school years there. I had

177

extremely low self-esteem. I always felt that nobody liked me, and I always worried about what everybody thought of me. I didn't have a lot of self-confidence.

I've read a ton of self-help books. I've gone to massive counseling to help build up my self-esteem. I come across as a powerhouse woman in real estate because I know what I'm doing. Now I coach hundreds of people, but I still fight my basic insecurity every day. That's why I continue to read self-help books, constantly discovering ways to gain more confidence. I learned that the more I believe in myself, the more I love myself, and the more positive thoughts I have, the better I am for myself and others. The second a negative thought comes into my head, I take it out. I literally say to myself, "That's not true," then I say something positive. One strategy I teach my students to use is to put a rubber band around their wrist. Anytime you say a negative thought to yourself, recognize it, then restate what you said into something positive and change the rubber band to the other wrist. You'll start to become more aware of the thoughts you are saying to yourself and become more aware. Being aware is the first step. Next you can start to change those internal voices and self-talk to become positive.

When I started in this business, I thought I had to be someone different. I thought that people weren't going to like me; that I talked too fast, that I was too hyper, and that no one was going to take me seriously. I thought I needed to come across serious and calm. (If you know me, you know how impossible that is. I wake up with more energy than the Energizer Bunny!)

You know what? Throughout the years, I've found the complete opposite. People love the fact that I have a lot of energy and talk fast. But my mind didn't believe this was true at first. I kept telling myself I needed to be more like this person or that person or that I wasn't enough just as I am. It took me a while to understand that this line of thinking was just a self-imposed obstacle. I didn't need to be someone else. I needed to believe in myself and see that people like me for who I am.

I also had to realize that if people don't like the fun, crazy Krista, then they aren't the people I'm trying to attract into my life. Yet, as confident as I've become, there is still the little inner voice that screams, "You're not good enough." I fight it daily and pay special attention to my thoughts. For years, people had been asking me to teach and train. They made comments like, "I wish I had your enthusiasm and drive. If you ever become a coach, I'd love for you to take me on." Back then, I never believed them.

Recently, I have been reading many books that tell you to listen to those subtle hints, take hold of them, grasp them, and go for it. That's probably one of the reasons you're reading this book. I had to learn to listen to the Universe that was pointing me in the direction of my calling: To be of service and add value to all that I can.

I didn't need to become someone else. I just needed to become a better version of me in some areas and stop thinking negatively. The second I stop believing in myself, whatever I'm going after is never going to happen. I try as hard as I can to have an attitude of, "I am doing this. This is working for me." I don't give myself the option that it is not going to work out. The actor Will Smith was once asked about his plan B if acting didn't work out. He said, "There is no reason to have a plan B because it distracts from plan A."

Today, I know there's nothing I can't achieve that I put my mind to. I know I need to work hard for my goals. They won't come for free and will not always be easy to achieve. I know I need to keep learning and implement what I learn until I've mastered it. But, as long as I keep applying myself and believing in myself, I know I can achieve just about anything. I remind myself of this frequently and you'll need to do the same. Research shows that this is one trait that most successful people have: They have the attitude and belief in themselves that they can do anything. If you don't have that belief in yourself, you need to work on it.

> *Research shows that this is one trait that most successful people have: They have the attitude and belief in themselves that they can do anything.*

We're so used to negative thoughts that we hardly recognize them. A very common one is, "Well, sure *she* can do it. But I'm not as talented/ smart/ energetic/ blah-dee blah blah blah." All you have to do is stand out and show your extraordinary value, and you can outshine that person over time. This won't happen overnight or even within a couple of months. But, once the momentum builds for you, especially using the power of social media and the internet, your business will take off.

However, if you don't believe it will or you truly believe that you can't do this, you might as well throw in the towel now. I just love this saying from Henry Ford: ***"Whether you think you can, or you think you can't—you're right."*** I just love that! Think you can because you can. It might feel easier to fall prey to your self-limiting beliefs. But the thoughts that say, "I can" and "I am" followed by something positive are the ones that will propel you forward.

Other negative statements I hear a lot are, "I can never learn the technology. I'm too old to learn the technology. I'm not good with computers." That's BS. I suck at computers. Honestly, I'm not the best at a lot of things. Things take a lot of time for me to learn, more than most. I was diagnosed with a learning disability in the second grade. I couldn't read. I'll never forget when I was in kindergarten and we had to memorize our phone number. I was the only kid that could not memorize it. Once you had it memorized, they'd give you this little fake phone key chain thingy. I wanted that keychain so bad! I'd try and try, and I just couldn't do it. Then at the end of the timeframe when we had to learn our phone numbers, they had this party. There was so much junk food, like being in Disneyland, but I didn't get to eat. I had to watch all the kids eating. I ended up getting held back from kindergarten (who can't pass that grade?). My point is that it takes me much longer than the average person to do and learn just about anything I attempt. But I know I can and will learn anything I put my mind to.

Like many of you, I'm not good at technology at all, but I studied, and I learned. Everything I do for my marketing, I learned by taking trainings and watching webinars. Using YouTube, you can learn to do almost anything. It was different ten years ago, but today you can find thousands of classes online to learn the technology you need. You just have to put the time and investment into learning. I am still constantly learning to be innovative and learning how I can use technology to stand out, be more efficient, and make a positive impact on my clients.

Certain programs and apps are easier than others. Figure out what the easier ones are and start there. Take it step by step, learning one app and implementing it into your business then learning another one. (In my Community Market Leader™ course, I teach every aspect of the technology you need.) I continue to add and implement as time changes because technology and innovations change. It's a constant!

Another limiting belief I've heard from coaching clients: "I don't have the time to do all of the things you're saying to do." My response is always, **"If you really want to have more time, if you really want to have more freedom, you'll make the time."** We can all make time for things that are important to us, right? By making a few adjustments in your life, like waking up an hour earlier and skipping your favorite TV shows, you'll find plenty of time to do those things that will give you so much more reward. "Limited time" is just another of those limiting beliefs, not the truth.

I always tell my students to look at their competitor, the one who is doing more business than they are. That person has the same amount of time in a day or year as you do. It's how they choose to spend that time that is giving them the competitive edge. We all have the same 24 hours. Check out the Pomodoro Technique (http://www. theultimatemarketingplaybook.com/member). It will save you massive amounts of time in your business if you actually are disciplined enough to use it.

Think about this: Once you take the time to do things differently and learn to generate leads and attract great clients more efficiently, you'll be thrilled you took the time to learn and implement new technologies. It's much better than going to ten thousand networking events or spending your weekends passing out flyers at auto shows or craft fairs. I don't know about you, but I'd much prefer going on a hike with my family or hitting up the Farmers' Market on Saturday.

My mind is not all gung-ho or in Pollyanna mode every day and every minute of the day. Like everybody, I have negative thoughts pop up. I've learned to notice that I'm having that negative thought or doubt, then I say something opposite. I'll say things like, "You're likable, you're enthusiastic, you speak clearly, you talk slowly, and you are totally calm (okay, this last one will never happen, but I can dream!)." And I'll say it with feeling, like I'm my own cheering squad, and drown out the noise of the negative stuff in my head. For help with this, I'd recommend reading books like: *I'm a Badass* by Jen Sincero, *Psycho-Cybernetics* by Maxwell Maltz, *Mindset: The New Psychology of Success* by Carol Dweck, *The Five Second Rule* by Mel Robbins, *How to Win Friends and Influence People* by Dale Carnegie, *Millionaire Success Habits* by Dean Graziosi, and one of my favorites *The Magic of Thinking Big* by David Schwartz.

Your Personal Advisory Team

"Real experts seek out constructive, even painful feedback. They're also skilled at understanding when and if a coach's advice doesn't work for them."
—Harvard Business Review July-August 2007

You don't have to create your success from scratch. Don't reinvent the world. Follow in the footsteps of someone who has the success you want. When people achieve great success, typically they've had a role model. They've emulated somebody who is already successful, studied what they did then copied those things. **You're in luck—you have me!** Though I'm not a loan officer or a financial planner, or a restaurant or a dance instructor, I've coached people in various businesses and professions to be highly successful. You just need to take the information in this book and *apply* it. That's the key to getting there, along with continuing to change and adapt.

Carol Delzer swears that every law school graduate who wants to start their own practice should get a business coach. "Even if their specialty is business law, when they get out of school, they don't have a clue how to put a practice together. I got a business coach early on and it made all the difference. My coach had knowledge and experience I didn't have. But even more importantly, she held me accountable."

Before he even started his own insurance brokerage, Glenn Hoffman created his own "brokers' college" for himself. "Because of the job I had when I started, I had connections with about 250 brokers throughout the Bay Area. I narrowed it down to 12 of the top brokers that I had the most respect for. As I worked with them, I interviewed them and asked tons of questions. I took them to lunch which basically became my classes. I learned all I could from them, and they were all happy to pass on what they knew."

Tracie Schmidt, a loan officer in my program, says, "I was already doing some of the things Krista recommends but I wasn't doing it effectively. For example, I'd been doing video probably for the last ten years in my business but just doing it here and there. In the last year and a half with Krista's training, I've taken the concept of doing video to a whole different level. Back then, no one was coaching me on video. Now I know how to do it the proper way and how to get it out to the community. And the results have been amazing. Doing video is great, but if you don't know how to properly distribute it, it won't make a dent in your business. That was also a huge part that I was missing. Now everywhere I go in my community, people recognize me." Tracie is now one of my accountability coaches in the program.

Please don't think that by reading this book, taking webinars, or attending classes, you'll instantly succeed and see dramatic changes in your business. To see change, you need to implement the practices and heed the advice you're given. You need to be accountable and the best way to do that is with a good coach. If you're not willing to do the work, then put this book down, run your business like the 96% of all the other businesses, professionals and service providers out there, and be satisfied with the results you get.

As I'm focusing on my training, and coaching business, I'm still running my real estate business selling homes. I have plenty of energy to do all of this because I'm so excited about it. It's exciting to learn! Implement what you've learned and start seeing the results.

As you continue to grow, you'll see how it really works. As you step into this process, and implement and master what I'm showing you, you'll feel that excitement, energy, and enthusiasm as well. You have the secret weapon: You have YOU!

Let's talk about mentors. I have mentors both in and outside of real estate and the training business, people I really want to emulate. There are certain people you want to emulate and others that you really should *not* emulate. Choose carefully. Make sure the people you emulate really have the type of success you want, those who will sincerely show you all you need to know and are authentically the kind of person you want to be. Ask a few questions in considering a mentor:

Do they really have the success you want? I'm guessing that there are several people out there who teach courses about succeeding in your industry, but they haven't really achieved that success themselves. They are more interested in succeeding by *teaching* success than succeeding in the business. Others have been in the business for decades. They still do things the way they did thirty years ago, or quite frankly even five years ago. They may still be productive because they've built a strong client base over the years. But they don't know how to build a business in today's market and they certainly don't know what it takes to become a Community Market Leader™. Make sure the people you're learning from have actually *done* what they're teaching you to do. Even better, they're currently doing it and doing it well.

You don't want to emulate the person who's doing just enough to get by until they're ready to retire. You certainly don't want to copy their habits if they're wandering into the office around 10:00 AM, chit-chatting on the phone for a few hours and doing the bare minimum for their clients. You don't want to emulate someone who is doing the business the way everyone else is doing it.

Instead, look for the person who stands out from the crowd. Emulate the person who is clearly professional at what they do and who is still passionate about their work and their clients. Model yourself after the person who is excited to learn new things and try different approaches. Imitate the other businesses and professionals in your industry who knows the business and profession inside and out, who admit when he doesn't know an answer then finds the answer. Choose the person who takes pride in the quality of everything they do, who treats every project like a million-dollar project and every client like their new best friend.

Are they sincerely offering what you need to know? In many businesses and professions, the first "mentor" you find is really just looking for a go-fer or free assistant. I ran into this myself. After my first year in real estate, I was very flattered when a top agent in the area asked me to partner with her. As I worked with her, I realized that she just wanted someone she could rely on to do all the work because she was planning to move. What I thought was a potential mentor turned out to be someone who took advantage of me.

Sometimes more experienced businesses and professionals want to help, but they're afraid of giving up "the secret sauce." They have some tricks up their sleeves that could really help you out, but they're afraid to share it. Make sure the person you choose as a mentor is generous with what they know. In fact, learn from someone who isn't in your area at all. Research the people who are top in your field around the country. See what they are doing, implement it, and do what they do *better*. If it's working for them, it can work for you. Don't ever stop, keep growing!

Are they the kind of person you want to be? Maybe you have a hot shot loan officer or insurance broker or architect who is willing to mentor you, but you sense that she isn't quite ethical in how she operates. Don't even go near her. Her reputation—which *will* get out no matter how clever she thinks she is—will taint you, as well.

Or maybe the best therapist around is a workaholic with no time for herself, her family, or her community. Working hard is one thing, but is that who you want to be? Most of us want success for the quality of life it can bring, not just to build up more money in our bank accounts than we could ever use.

I mentioned Tony Robbins earlier. I've been to many of his events and read his books. I look at him and see his compassion, empathy, and drive to help everybody. He's amazing at what he does. He's innovative in his thoughts and techniques, and he just goes for it. He is knowledgeable about so many things, from how to make and keep your money to personal self-help. He goes above and beyond with everything he does in his life, from giving back, to supporting charities, to feeding the homeless. He's a total giver. In fact, my affirmation is, "I want to be the female Tony Robbins. I want to help as many people succeed as I can. I will positively affect every life I touch. The more I give, the more I get. I positively attract anything and everything I need into my business to be a complete success."

I sat in one of his four-day training events with my husband and my then-fifteen-year-old and eighteen-year-old daughters. Each day was anywhere from twelve to eighteen hours, and we were totally engaged and energized the entire time. This guy has apparently made around $440 million, yet when he's up there you can tell he's sincere about wanting to help people, wanting to change lives, and wanting to do things for the right reasons.

There were over ten thousand people at that particular event, and he gave us each a book. It's called *Money: Master the Game*, and I'd encourage everyone to read it. This book isn't just some throw-away that you can read in two hours. It has a lot of valuable content that you can apply. When I am writing my books, my goal is always to give that same kind of value.

I have used different coaches to help me structure my business, improve my public speaking skills, improve as a leader, learn funnels and digital marketing, and work on personal growth and development. I started working with each of them because they resonate so well with me. Some helped me set boundaries with my clients and have worked with me on how I speak to people and the language I use. Another business coach is teaching me how to tell a story on stage, and how to speak clearly and have confidence when I'm on stage. The Tony Robbins Coaching Program is helping me both personally as well as with time management in my business. I'm working with a business coach to learn how to build a business that gives you a lifestyle of freedom in two years or less. I'm also coaching with a man who helps you *ethically* persuade people to take action they already want to take and that is really in their best interests, but fear holds them back. His focus (and mine) is making sure people are not pressured into something that ultimately isn't good for them but that you help them overcome fears and take steps that will benefit them.

Not all coachers are going to work for you. I met one coach at seminar where someone else was the primary speaker. She gave a 20-minute presentation and I was totally impressed. She got up on stage and spoke clearly, effectively, and with authority. I felt like she was talking directly to me. I didn't even have to think about it. I immediately signed up for her course. She resonated more with me in her 20-minute presentation than the person who put on the event and who spoke for the majority of the three days. She showed up like a leader. She was a powerhouse, seemed to know her stuff, and was confident.

However, once I got into her program, I realized that she seemed more interested in the money than in the students. I also realized I knew a lot more than she did about marketing. I ended up fulfilling the contract I had with her but chose not to continue with studying her material. I didn't beat myself up over it, I just chalked it up to life and moved on.

So, find a mentor or coach that you resonate with, not only what they teach but who they are.

An Environment That Supports Your Success

Maybe even more important than a coach is the environment you live in. This is about all the people you hang out with on a regular basis. It's great to touch base with someone who will cheer you on and give you good tips a couple of times a month. But if the people you see and interact with on a daily basis are doom and gloom Negative Nellies, it will be tough to keep your momentum moving forward. Does this mean you need to ditch the friends you've had since kindergarten? Maybe, but that's up to you and it depends on how much negative influence they have on you. At the very least, you want to identify the people that are sucking the juice and enthusiasm out of you and minimize your time around them. You also don't want to share your most cherished dreams and goals with that kind of person. They'll only try to pop holes in your balloon. Instead, you want to surround yourself with people who are positive and going after their own goals and dreams so you can be a cheering squad for each other. And if you don't have friends like this? You need to find some! Check out different organizations in your community like Rotary Clubs and Toastmasters groups. They often cater to people who are heading forward in life, not moaning about the past and what "can't" be done.

Environment also means you need to pay attention to what you let into your brain. It's too easy to watch the news and feel hopeless about the world. It's too easy to hear a rotten economic forecast and start to believe that your success will be impossible in a weak economy (which in my experience is NOT true!). Instead you want to fill your brain with positive and hopeful news and stories. And if you look in the right places, there's plenty of it! So be conscious of the books you read, the podcasts you listen to, even the Facebook posts you skim, and the TV shows you watch. Negative messages can sabotage you and weaken your commitment.

A 2005 article by Alan Deutschman called "Change or Die" talked about heart patients who were told that if they did not change their lifestyle, they would die. Still, after just one year, 90% of the people went back to their old lifestyles. Another researcher took a similar group of patients with clogged arteries and told them the lifestyle changes they needed to make. But these patients were attending group support meetings twice a week. After three years, 77% of this group had successfully kept to their lifestyle changes. The difference? They had a supportive environment where they held each other accountable and discussed challenges. So, you are seven times more likely to make a change in the right environment with the right people.

Constant Education

We talked about education to increase your expertise in your industry and to stay current with your business, professional trends and your market. But, to succeed as a Community Market Leader™, you need to go beyond that. You need to step out of your industry and focus on getting better at a number of things. Maybe you need to become a better public speaker. Maybe you need to increase your confidence. Maybe you need to learn to handle your finances more intelligently or responsibly. **We all have areas that need improving.**

I did so much work in real estate for 15 years that I felt like I left my own personal growth and development behind. Over the past few years, I've started focusing on that area. My goal is to enhance my speaking skills and coaching skills so I can make an even bigger impact. I am constantly listening to motivational podcasts and reading uplifting books.

Find those areas where you can improve and make a plan. Stay in a learning mode *always* so that expanding your knowledge is a consistent theme in your life. Challenge yourself to become better at something every single week.

> *Stay in a learning mode always so that expanding your knowledge is a consistent theme in your life.*

It really is about the journey. I know we all want to reach our goals but at the end of the day, we need to appreciate every single step we take toward them. Think about an Olympic athlete. They train for years and years just to perform for a few minutes on the gymnastics floor or sprint for less than a minute. When you win the gold medal, the success and wins are not when you cross the finish line, but when you got up every single day and swam when it was 20 degrees outside or when you did another lap around the track even though you're exhausted. It was when you left a party early or don't go at all because you need to get up early and hit the gym. The real win was when you sacrificed to get better at what you do or to become a better person. That's where all the winning comes. Those are your biggest wins, not when you get the gold medal. It's who you have become to get there that is the biggest prize. In doing all they did, those Olympic athletes become different people. They become disciplined, more self-confident, and develop positive mindsets. They get smarter about their sport and get guidance from the best coaches in the world. Maybe they won the gold or maybe they didn't. But what they gained is even more important. I want this for you too.

The most important thing is having a mindset of "I can do this. This is working for me. I am achieving my goals." To me, this mindset is the number one thing that determines success. I make sure it shows up in every move I make. For example, when I was building my house, I didn't want to get a loan for it because if I got a loan, it would mean that I didn't believe in myself. To me, getting a loan meant that I was doubting I could achieve enough success in my coaching business to pay for it. My husband and parents kept saying "Just get a loan. Alleviate all the stress." But I knew if I got the loan, I'd be sabotaging my mindset and my goals in a way. I built the house with not having to ever get a loan. All of the success I have has come from focusing on my mindset as much anything else—and working on it constantly.

It's what you gain along the way that is most important. Getting your specific goals is awesome. Yet who you have to become on the journey toward those goals will make a huge impact on all areas of your life. Take the time to notice how you're changing and improving and give yourself a pat on the back for all the effort you're putting into the journey.

Staying Energized

To become and continue to be a Community Market Leader™ takes a lot of energy. Rather than taking the minimum requirement of continuing education, Community Market Leaders® are educating themselves on a weekly basis then implementing what they're learning. Community Market Leaders® aren't content with their last good idea, they're constantly improving month after month on what they're producing. They ask, "How can I make this better for my clients and the community I serve? How can I give even more value?" They constantly test to find out what's working and what's not. Their business is constantly evolving based upon new technologies and innovations. And, because they're doing all of that, their business is growing exponentially.

It takes a lot of energy and energy comes from enthusiasm.

I want you to be enthusiastic about becoming a Community Market Leader™, not just going along for the ride. I want you to be enthusiastic as you're learning, and enthusiastic when you're implementing. Be enthusiastic when something doesn't work because it's teaching you what does. I always say, "Appreciate when you feel overwhelmed because it means that you're learning and growing." Be enthusiastic about even the smallest of gains. If you're not usually an enthusiastic kind of person, work on that. It will bring you amazing rewards. I think one of the reasons I've been so successful in my careers has a lot to do with my enthusiasm. People can see that I truly care about what I'm doing and I'm passionate about what I teach and my students' success. The more enthusiastic and passionate you are about what you do and the people that you serve, everyone will be able to see it and feel it. You'll attract more business from the clients you really want to work with.

> *"Appreciate when you feel overwhelmed because it means that you're learning and growing."*

I don't wake up happy every single day. When I was going through my divorce, I was so sad, lonely, angry and panicked. I'll never forget one morning on the first Thanksgiving that my daughters were at their dad's (my ex-husband's). The house was empty and quiet. I just sat in the kitchen alone and crying. Just weeks prior my family had been ripped apart and I felt like there was no hope. I missed them so much my heart hurt. I felt very sorry for myself. It was tough, but I still tried my hardest to be as positive as I could and show up with enthusiasm. I put a happy face on, and I continue to do that every day. I faked it until I made it.

Sometimes some of the hardest times in our life end up giving us the happiest of results. At the time, I was devastated. But looking back, it was meant to happen. I've met my husband Steve, and he's my one and only. We are best friends and he is one of the most loyal men I know (right next to my Dad). I am so thankful for everything that happened and looking back I think I was just in love with the "idea" of being married. But the marriage I was in back then wasn't that great at all. In fact, I know if I'd stayed married, I'd not be who I am today. I think my spark would have blown out long ago. I know for certain I would not have written any of my books or have had the ability to coach, I would have been to worn down.

I still have rough days, but it's how I choose to approach these days that counts. It's how I show up. I'm an Audible nut, I love listening to books all the time. I go back and forth between them. I listened to *How to Master the Art of Selling* by Tom Hopkins. He says that in any business and profession, we will always have challenges. We need to welcome challenges and should be grateful for them because that means it offers an obstacle to overcome. He reminds us that in life we are going to hear "no" more than once.

We are going to see a loan we thought for sure was going to be ours go to another loan officer. We are going to see a perfect student go to a different yoga studio. We're going to have our awesome renovation plan rejected for someone else's. We're going to lose students to another program. If it hasn't happened to you yet, it will. Buck up. You will not get every single job or client. Just learn and grow from the challenges and move on. There is no power at all in regret, shame or guilt. Just ask if you could have done anything differently or better, then do that next time. Not everyone is going to connect with you and that's okay. We can't win them all! And, from what I've learned, we don't want to. I've learned that there is a reason you didn't get that customer or client. It wasn't in *your* best interest in the first place.

You have to show that you love what you're doing. Being enthusiastic is basically being in love with people, being in love with your job, being in love with serving your clients. That's enthusiasm. I love what I do, and I love people. Clients can hear that in my voice and in how I speak with them. I am not just in it for the money. Yes, like just about everyone I like money, but money comes because I place people before things, always. The money then always follows. And please, love what you do. My quote for business is, "When You Do What You Love, People Love What You Do!"

> "When You Do What You Love, People Love What You Do!"

Believe U Can

When I started putting together my training and coaching programs, I came up with an acronym to help people remember the most important parts of being a Community Market Leader™. It's Believe U Can and here's how I've broken it down:

Believe: To succeed at this or just about anything in life, you need to get your head straight and keep it straight. This means noticing when your thoughts wander into negativity and cutting them off at the pass. This means infusing your brain with positive teachings from teachers like Napoleon Hill or Dale Carnegie. This means not buying into your self-doubts or letting any negative circumstance determine your attitude. You get what you think about. Think and know that you can do or be anything you want. You are the only person that can get you there or who can stop you from getting there. One of my famous lines to my students is, "If you keep doing what you've always done, you'll always get the same result. We have to change our actions to get the desired result we are looking for."

Another one of my favorite books is *You Are A Badass* by Jen Sincero. The tagline is *How to Stop Doubting Your Greatness and Start Living an Awesome Life*. She teaches that you can do anything no matter what it is, but you need to believe it. The book is very similar to *Think and Grow Rich*, but a little easier to understand (especially for teens). Also, *The Five Second Rule* by Mel Robbins is a book that will help you reach your goals, achieve anything you desire and overcome any obstacle you may be experiencing.

"There is one quality which one must possess to win, and that is definiteness of purpose, the knowledge of what one wants, and a burning desire to possess it."
—*Napoleon Hill*

Educate: Be an educator, not a self-promoter. First become a true expert, then share your expertise. Give people in your community information that will keep them abreast of what's happening in the world of your business or your profession. Give your clients information that will help them make good decisions in life. Be the go-to person for anyone who wants to know about your expertise. Show your community all the knowledge you have, share it with them. This is what sets you up to be seen as a leader and an authority.

"Education is for improving the lives of others and for leaving your community and the world better than you found it."
—*Marian Wright Edelman*

Learn: To educate others, you first have to learn enough to be a true authority and expert—and keep learning. Tap into the knowledge of mentors and coaches. Study critical areas and trends of your business and profession. Improve in areas where you're weak by taking classes, webinars, and workshops. Learning should never stop, we need to constantly learn, improve, and add to our piggy bank of knowledge.

"An investment in knowledge pays the best interest."
— *Benjamin Franklin*

Innovate: Be different! Stay in the mode of creating new ways of doing things. Use technology to reach more people, be more efficient, and get better results. Don't stick with "the ways we've always done it." Many industries have tried to avoid change over the past couple of decades, but like all of us, they have to change to survive. Find new, better, and more efficient ways of doing *everything* and never stop doing this. When everyone else is doing ABC, you do PDQ, and do it with a BANG!!

"If you always do what you've always done, you'll always get what you've always gotten."
—attributed to Mark Twain, Henry Ford, Tony Robbins

Engage/Everywhere: Engage your community by offering them valuable information that is relevant to them. Engage them by using video so they can feel a more personal connection. Be everywhere using social media and the internet with your informational videos, ads and marketing. Let people know you before they meet you. Get personal with them. You'll see how powerful this is and how quickly you'll see the results. Engagement is equal to connection, and connection is so powerful. Think about the dynamics with your family and friends. You've built a strong connection that keeps you close. This will help you to earn trust, respect and be looked upon as a leader.

"Communication—the human connection—is the key to personal and career success."
—Paul J. Meyer

Value: Give real value in everything you do. Go so far above and beyond for your clients that they are thrilled to work with you. Constantly ask, "What more can I do to serve?" People are mainly concerned with themselves and what you can do for them. How can you help them? What's in it for them? Always focus on what you can *give* them. Also, stick to your own values and be impeccably ethical in all you do.

"Earn your success based on service to others, not at the expense of others."
—H. Jackson Brown, Jr.

Energy/Enthusiasm: Love what you do! Tackle every project, every class, every contract as if it's your favorite thing to do. Show up with confidence that you'll do an outstanding job. Answer the phone with a smile. Show the world that you love life, you love them, and you love what you do!

> *"When you do what you love, people love what you do."*
> —Krista Mashore

> *"Flaming enthusiasm, backed up by horse sense and persistence, is the quality that most frequently makes for success."*
> —Dale Carnegie

Unique: Seek to stand out from the crowd and be different in all you do. Capitalize on your gifts and share them with the world. Being unique is what makes you memorable. If you do things like everyone else, you'll blend in and get lost in the shuffle. A CML® doesn't just blend in with the crowd. Your unique personal qualities and business practices will help you lead in your field.

> *"What sets you apart can sometimes feel like a burden and it's not. And a lot of the time, it's what makes you great."*
> —Emma Stone

Courageous: Be bold and persistent. Do whatever it takes to serve your clients and reach your goals, even if it scares the heck out of you. Take each failure, learn what it can teach you, then try again. Your dreams are totally attainable. They just need a timeline and a series of smaller goals attached to them. Right now, I am pursuing my dream. I have to tell you, by doing this I am truly happier now then I've ever been. I feel so content and satisfied. I'm generally a very happy person, but it's now at a different level. I am happier in my marriage than ever before, and in my relationships with my children, friends, and peers. When you're bold enough to go after your dreams and what inspires you, it makes you show up differently in life.

> *"All our dreams can come true, if we have the courage to pursue them."*
> —Walt Disney

Articulate/Action: Learn to express yourself to your community and your clients. Communicate clearly and with patience, remembering that others don't have your expertise. Articulate your appreciation. And take action! Make a plan to achieve your goals and act on that plan. Be sure to implement what you learn. Work it, tweak it, adjust what you are doing and keep making it better and better. If you learn something and it doesn't work, that's okay. You will fail a few times. Get back up and eventually you'll find something that is a home run.

> *"Create a definite plan for carrying out your desire and begin at once, whether you are ready or not, to put this plan into action."*
>
> —*Napoleon Hill*

Niche: Don't try to be everything to everyone. Focus your business on the niche that fits you best. Learn what you need to learn to succeed in that niche. You don't have to be all things to all people. Look at what you enjoy, what you want to specialize in, and be laser focused on that. Perfect that one area and capitalize on it.

> *"Identify your niche and dominate it. And when I say dominate, I just mean work harder than anyone else could possibly work at it."*
>
> —*Nate Parker*

Two Final Keys: Gratitude and Persistence

I am a big believer in the power of gratitude. Research shows that gratitude is not just something for Sunday school or people who have watched *The Secret*. A recent Harvard Medical School article stated, "gratitude is strongly and consistently associated with greater happiness. Gratitude helps people feel more positive emotions, relish good experiences, improve their health, deal with adversity, and build strong relationships."

We get caught up in pursuing our goals and wanting to be better, more prosperous, and successful. There's nothing wrong with that. However, while we're doing that, it is important to be grateful for what we already have and who we already are—everything in our lives. Even if you're struggling financially, odds are that you are doing better than 93% of the world's population. And, more importantly, you have the opportunities to turn that around. Be grateful for that.

Be grateful that you ran into this book. I've offered you so many tools that will truly make a difference in your business and your life. Treat the knowledge I've shared as the gift it is and take action on it. Be grateful for whatever level of health, prosperity, and community connections you have. Marchall Sylver wrote, *"When you look for what's working in your life, it expands."*

Take nothing for granted—your family, your friends, your opportunities, your well-being. Appreciate the life you've been given and all that you've experienced. If you feel inclined to whine and complain about something, knock it off! Wallowing in regrets or "if only's" never got anyone anywhere. Step into the attitude of gratitude and notice what a difference it makes. I read somewhere that a person's biggest regrets are the ones that they know they can still do something about but still choose not to. So don't let that be you.

And be persistent.

You might have read some of my suggestions and thought, "Oh, that's way out of my comfort zone. I could never do that." Well, yes, you can. Keep your "why" in front of you as you continue to learn and take action on what you're learning. If you keep on doing what you've always done, you'll keep on getting what you've always gotten.

Often, as you're about to master something new or you're very close to the end result you want, that's exactly when it gets the toughest. Many people back off when their business is just about to turn the corner. Don't stop. Keep on going.

I'm happy pursuing my dream of being a coach and trainer, but that doesn't mean that it's been an easy road. I have had more trials and tribulations lately than I've had in years. But I know it's the storm before the sky clears and the sun pops out again. It's the palm tree that is bent over during the hurricane that, once it finally bounces back, it's stronger than before the storm. It's the caterpillar that turned into a cocoon, thinking about how lonely and dark and crammed it is in the cocoon. But after time of being all crammed up, dark and lonely, the caterpillar turns into a beautiful butterfly that can fly rather than having to crawl. I know that when things get rough it's because they are about to be better than ever, but NOT if I give up. Dale Carnegie *Think and Grow Rich* talks about a man who got discouraged and stopped mining for gold. A garbage man bought the mining machine from him for pennies on the dollar and hired someone to study the ground to figure out where the gold was. It was just *three feet* from where the first man had stopped. The garbage man made millions.

When Winston Churchill had to lead Great Britain through World War II, he often had to encourage his country to never give up despite terrible setbacks. He said, *"Success consists of going from failure to failure without loss of enthusiasm."* Dale Carnegie wrote, *"A quitter never wins, and a winner never quits."* And there's a Japanese proverb that says, *"Nanakorobi yaoki,"* which means, *"Fall down seven times and stand up eight."* Anyone who has achieved success will tell you that you just need to keep putting one foot in front of the other, no matter what.

Thank you for spending your precious time reading this book. I hope you will use what I've shared to achieve all you desire. I'd love to hear some of your thoughts and success, just #CommunityMarketLeader or #KristaMashoreCoaching and I'll be sure to see them.

Sincerely,

Krista Mashore

For more information on becoming a Community Market Leader™ go to www.KristaMashore.com

Take the Next Step

1. *Think about your current mindset. How strong is it? What do you need to improve in it? How much do you believe that you can succeed? How much does your current environment support you? What thoughts might hold you back? Write all of this down.*

2. *Next, think of some ways to improve your mindset. Is it finding a good coach? Signing up for webinars? Changing something (or someone) in your environment? Come up with three things you can do now to strengthen your mindset and schedule a time to implement them.*

RESOURCES

You have access to many resources to support you on your journey to becoming a highly successful Community Market Leader™! My website at KristaMashoreCoaching.com has a ton of free videos, templates, and trainings.

Here are some other resources I mentioned:

BombBomb: for video messages (mention Krista Mashore)

Rev.com: for transcriptions

Trint.com: for transcriptions

ClickFunnels (KristaMashore.com/clickfunnels)

SoTellUs (www.SoTellUs.com/Krista)

Books I Recommend

Here's a list of books that have been particularly important to me. Some are classics and some are more recent. Personally, I use audio books, so I have a constant stream of good information and inspiration.

Expert Secrets, Dotcom Secrets and Traffic Secrets by Russell Brunson

Think and Grow Rich by Napoleon Hill

How to Win Friends and Influence People by Dale Carnegie

You Are A Badass by Jen Sincero

Never Lose a Customer Again by Joey Coleman

Mindset: The New Psychology of Success by Carol Dweck

The Power of Consistency by Weldon Long

Psycho-Cybernetics by Maxwell Maltz

The 12 Week Year: Get More Done in 12 Weeks Than Others Do in 12 Months by Brian P. Moran

Millionaire Success Habits by Dean Graziosi

The Go Giver by Bob Berg and John David Mann

The 5 Second Rule: Transform your Life, Work, and Confidence with Everyday Courage by Mel Robbins

The Ultimate Sales Machine by Chet Holmes

The Success Principles by Jack Canfield

Extreme Ownership by Jocko Willink and Leif Babin

The Conversion Code by Chris Smith

For more information on becoming a Community Market Leader™ go to www.KristaMashore.com

Notes

Notes

Notes

Notes

Notes

Notes

Notes

Notes

Notes

Notes